WITHDRAWN

As one of the world's longest established
and best-known travel brands,
Thomas Cook are the experts in travel.

For more than 135 years ou~
guidebooks have unlock
of destinations arou
sharing with travelle~
experience and a passi

Rely on Thomas C
travelling companion on you~ next trip
and benefit from our unique heritage.

Thomas Cook **traveller** guides

WARSAW
Christian Swindells

Thomas
Cook

Your travelling companion since 1873

Written and updated by Christian Swindells, after an original manuscript by
Liliana Olchowik-Adamowska and Tomasz Ławecki

Published by Thomas Cook Publishing
A division of Thomas Cook Tour Operations Limited
Company registration no. 3772199 England
The Thomas Cook Business Park, Unit 9, Coningsby Road,
Peterborough PE3 8SB, United Kingdom
Email: books@thomascook.com, Tel: + 44 (0) 1733 416477
www.thomascookpublishing.com

Produced by Cambridge Publishing Management Limited
Burr Elm Court, Main Street, Caldecote CB23 7NU
www.cambridgepm.co.uk

ISBN: 978-1-84848-345-3

Series Editor: Karen Beaulah
Production/DTP: Steven Collins

Printed and bound in Spain by GraphyCems

Cover photography: © Barbara Santoro/SIME-4Corners Images Ltd

Contents

Introduction

The official symbol of Warsaw is a mermaid armed with sword and shield, although given the city's history a phoenix would probably be a more appropriate choice. Invaded, occupied, burnt, blown up and generally destroyed on numerous occasions, the city has always survived and continues to attract visitors who appreciate its complexity. After the dark days of Nazi occupation and 45 long years of communism, Warsaw is now the dynamic capital of the powerhouse of new Europe.

Warsaw has long been Poland's political, economic and cultural capital. It attracts the best and the brightest of young Poles, eager to make their mark in whatever field they choose. But not many people can trace their roots here more than a couple of generations back. Virtually all the citizens of Warsaw were either expelled or killed during World War II. Wander around the Old Town (Stare Miasto) and you can hardly believe that more than 90 per cent of the buildings have been entirely rebuilt since 1945. In 1980 UNESCO placed the Old Town on the list of World Heritage sites as 'an outstanding example of a near-total reconstruction of a span of history covering the 13th to the 20th century'.

Not everything has been built as beautifully as the Old Town. The prefabricated tower blocks that make up the suburbs of Ursynów, and even dot the city centre as the Żelazna Brama development, are far from attractive and are rapidly reaching the end of the lifespan they were designed for. The first line of the Metro and its 21 stations have taken some 24 years to build. The Palace of Culture and Science (*see pp30–31*) is widely regarded as an eyesore, and many older Varsovians (inhabitants of Warsaw) would be glad to see it pulled down. Yet even this relic of communism shows how Warsaw makes the best of any opportunity. In 1989 the 40 floors of office space immediately became the hub of capitalism in Poland.

The Warsaw of the 21st century is a city that's changing fast but is still proudly holding on to its history. Fifteen years ago there was not even one nightclub, and shopping was best done at an outdoor market at the abandoned national stadium. Nowadays the clubs are packed until well past dawn and two of central Europe's largest retail investments are in the city centre. Nonetheless, walk past many of the buildings that remained standing in 1945 and you'll see bullet holes in the stone.

Warsaw has consistently been exactly the wrong place at the wrong time but it has never failed to do the right thing. In many ways, it's a symbol of the entire nation of Poland: often defeated but never cowed and never broken. Rebuilding Warsaw was a matter of national pride. Varsovians don't waste time looking back in anger; they're too busy looking forward to an ever brighter future. Mottos usually state what a company, family or city would like to be. Warsaw is different and so is its motto: *Semper invicta* – Always invincible – is simply a statement of what Warsaw is.

The Market Square (the Rynek), in Warsaw's rebuilt Old Town

The city

When luck was being handed out, the capital of Poland wasn't even at the back of the queue. Instead, Warsaw was making sure it got double helpings of energy and imagination for its citizens. Crises come, crises go, large sections of the city are violently destroyed every half a century or so, but Warsaw clings on stubbornly to both banks of the Vistula River no matter what cruel fortune or the fates can throw at it.

Warsaw lies at 52 degrees, 15 minutes north and exactly 21 degrees east. This location puts it in the heart of the Mazovian plain, which was largely created by the Scandinavian ice sheet during the last Ice Age. The ice sheet can take the credit for what passes for soil in this area: sandy, fluvial deposits on a layer of clay; barely fertile and distinctly problematic to build on. Poland itself is, generally speaking, one large plain with Warsaw in the middle of it and is surrounded by countries that have historically been considerably more powerful. Hence the rather unkind but almost entirely accurate description of the country as 'a field in search of a battle'; over its troubled past, numerous invading armies have paid regular visits to rape, pillage and plunder, and Warsaw, as the capital, has borne the brunt of this. This is not a location where a city would be expected to survive, let alone to thrive. But Warsaw isn't just any city; like the people who live here, this city delights

in ducking and diving, dodging and weaving, beating the odds and defying predictions. Leave your preconceived ideas at home: the 'Big Potato' is the kind of place where you can confidently expect the unexpected.

Early beginnings

The first settlement in what is now Warsaw was Bródno, on the eastern bank of the Vistula, which dates back to the 9th century. Jazdów was the first settlement on the left bank, founded in the 12th century. The name Warszawa first appeared in the 13th century when the castle at Jazdów was raided by Lithuanian forces in 1281 and a new settlement was set up by the Duke of Mazovia on a site now occupied by the Royal Castle, next to a fishing village named Warszowa. There's a legend that the village was founded by a fisherman named Wars and his wife Sawa, but Warszowa actually means 'owned by Warsz': Warsz was the name of the family that owned the land around modern-day Mariensztat. In 1413 the Duke moved his capital down the river from Czersk to Warsaw. Later in that century the path of the Vistula River shifted, leaving Czersk about 2km (1¼ miles) away from the river. This accident of fluvial geography ensured that Warsaw became the most important city in Mazovia, and in 1526 it became the capital of the newly created province of Mazovia, a part of the Kingdom of Poland.

Kraków was still the capital of Poland but Warsaw's importance was growing, and, after the 1569 formation of the Polish-Lithuanian Commonwealth, it was decided to hold the Grand *Sejm* (the parliament) exclusively in Warsaw.

The monarchy

After the death of the last of the Jagiellonian kings, Zygmunt Augustus II, in 1572, Poland introduced the idea of

Mariensztat: once Warszowa, cradle of Warsaw

elected monarchy. European princes would be elected king of Poland at a special electoral field in the village of Wielka Wola (now a district of Warsaw). The third king elected there was Zygmunt III, a descendant of both the Polish Jagiellonian and Swedish Vasa dynasties. In 1596, nine years after his election, a fire in the Royal Castle in Kraków prompted Zygmunt to temporarily move his official residence to Warsaw castle and then to announce that Warsaw would be his permanent residence.

This relocation of the royal court prompted the building of numerous palaces and luxurious residences in and around Warsaw, as well as an increase in the number of inhabitants. But being a capital city wasn't always easy: between 1665 and 1668 Warsaw was besieged three times by a joint Swedish-Transylvanian army, and on each occasion it was captured and pillaged. Much of the city was destroyed and the vast majority of its cultural and historical objects were lost. Yet the city survived, and by the rule of Jan III Sobieski (1674–96) was unquestionably the leading city in Poland. The years 1674–1792 marked the second golden age of Warsaw. A considerable number of palaces were built in the classical style and the city became the centre of the Polish enlightenment. In 1743 the world's first free public library was opened in Warsaw, and in 1773 the first national education ministry in the world was set up here.

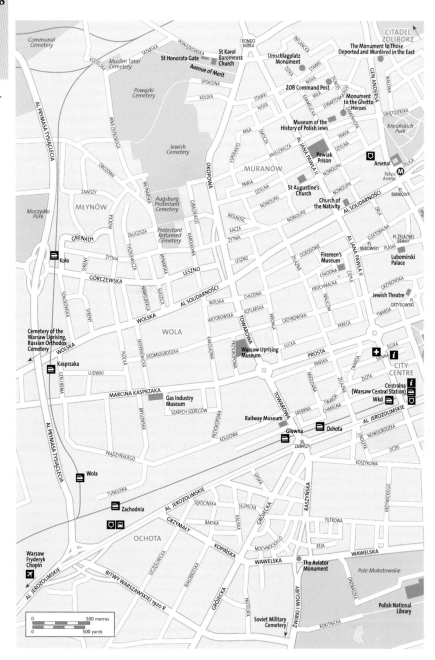

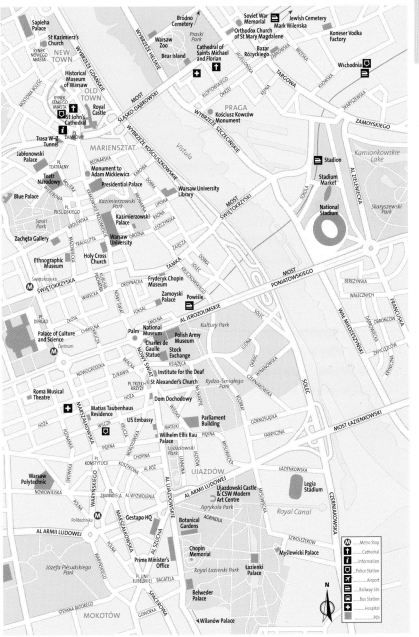

Sapieha Palace
St Kazimierz's Church
RYNEK NOWEGO MIASTA
NEW TOWN
WYBRZEŻE GDAŃSKIE
Bródno Cemetery
Praski Park
Warsaw Zoo
Bear Island
Soviet War Memorial
Mark Wilenska
Orthodox Church of St Mary Magdalene
Jewish Cemetery
Koneser Vodka Factory
MOSTOWA BOLEŚĆ
Historical Museum of Warsaw
RYNEK STAREGO MIASTA
OLD TOWN
St John's Cathedral
Royal Castle
MOST ŚLĄSKO-DĄBROWSKI
Cathedral of Saints Michael and Florian
KŁOPOTOWSKIEGO
OKRZEI
JAGIELLOŃSKA
KĘPNA
PRAGA
TARGOWA
Wschodnia
SKARŻYŃSKA
ZAMOYSKIEGO

Trasa W-Z Tunnel
PL ZAMKOWY
Jabłonowski Palace
PL TEATRALNY
MARIENSZTAT
BEDNARSKA
Monument to Adam Mickiewicz
Presidential Palace
Vistula
Kościusz Kowców Monument
WYBRZEŻE SZCZECIŃSKIE
WYBRZEŻE KOŚCIUSZKOWSKIE
Kamionkowskie Lake

Teatr Narodowy
WIERZBOWA
FOCHA
Blue Palace
PL PIŁSUDSKIEGO
Saski Park
Zachęta Gallery
KRÓLEWSKA
MAZOWIECKA
TRAUGUTTA
KRAKOWSKIE PRZEDMIEŚCIE
Kazimierzowski Park
Kazimierzowski Palace
Warsaw University
Warsaw University Library
BROWARNA
LIPOWA
OBOŻNA
RADNA
LESZCZYŃSKA
ZAJĘCZA
MOST ŚWIĘTOKRZYSKI
Stadion
Stadium Market
National Stadium
Skaryszewski Park
AL ZIELENIECKA
SOKOLA

Ethnographic Museum
Świętokrzyska
ŚWIĘTOKRZYSKA
Holy Cross Church
KUBUSIA PUCHATKA
ORDYNACKA
NOWY ŚWIAT
WARECKA
Fryderyk Chopin Museum
Zamoyski Palace
Powiśle
TAMKA
SOLEC
DOBRA
KRUCZKOWSKIEGO
MOST PONIATOWSKIEGO
BEREZYŃSKA
WALECZNYCH
WAŁ MIEDZESZYŃSKI
FRANCISZKA
DĄBRÓWKI
OBROŃCÓW

PL DEFILAD
ZŁOTA
CHMIELNA
FOKSAL
SMOLNA
AL JEROZOLIMSKIE
Kultury Park
SOLEC
ZWYCIĘZCÓW
KRYNICZNA

Palace of Culture and Science
Centrum
NONOGRODZKA
BRACKA
ŻURAWIA
Palm
National Museum
Charles de Gaulle Statue
Polish Army Museum
Stock Exchange
KSIĄŻĘCA
Institute for the Deaf
NOWY ŚWIAT
Rydza-Śmigłego Park
NA SKARPIE
CZERNIAKOWSKA
LUDNA
OKRĄG
ROZBRAT
WINAKOWSKA
WAŁ MIEDZESZYŃSKI

Roma Musical Theatre
MARSZAŁKOWSKA
PL TRZECH KRZYŻY
St Alexander's Church
HOŻA
Dom Dochodowy
WILCZA
Matias Taubenhaus Residence
HOŻA
POZNAŃSKA
US Embassy
MATEJKI
Wilhelm Ellis Rau Palace
PIĘKNA
Parliament Building
WIEJSKA
GÓRNOŚLĄSKA
FABRYCZNA
MOST ŁAZIENKOWSKI

PIĘKNA
KRUCZA
KOSZYKOWA
CHOPINA
Ujazdowski Park
MYŚLIWIECKA
AŻIENKOWSKA
ŁAZIENKOWSKA
Legia Stadium

Warsaw Polytechnic
NOWOWIEJSKA
PL KONSTYTUCJI
AL RÓŻ
UJAZDÓW
JAZDÓW
AL UJAZDOWSKIE
AL ARMII LUDOWEJ
Ujazdowski Castle & CSW Modern Art Centre
Royal Canal
CZERNIAKOWSKA

Politechnika
POLNA
WARYŃSKIEGO
PL ZBAWICIELA
AL WYZWOLENIA
Gestapo HQ
AGRYKOLA
Agrykola Park
ŁAZIENKOWSKA

AL ARMII LUDOWEJ
Botanical Gardens
AL SZUCHA
MARSZAŁKOWSKA

Józefa Piłsudskiego Park
WARYŃSKIEGO
POLNA
Prime Minister's Office
PL UNII LUBELSKIEJ
BAGATELA
Chopin Memorial
Royal Łazienki Park
SZWOLEŻERÓW
Łazienki Palace
Myślewicki Palace

MOKOTÓW
STEFANA BATOREGO
SPACEROWA
GOWORKA
Belweder Palace
Wilanów Palace

N

Metro Stop
Cathedral
Information
Police Station
Airport
Railway Stn
Bus Station
Hospital
POI

Occupation and rebellion

The partition of about a third of Poland between Russia, Prussia and Austria in 1772 led to Warsaw being occupied by foreign troops, but it brought a characteristic response from Varsovians: 1789 saw the city's leading citizens march from the Market Square to the Royal Castle to present the king with a list of reforms that Poland needed. This led to the Polish government publishing the Constitution of 3 May 1791, Europe's first modern constitution. With hindsight that may not have been the wisest of moves; Russia invaded in May 1792 and, with Prussia, seized yet more Polish territory, captured Warsaw again and stationed a sizeable garrison in the city. That garrison met with a sticky end: in April 1794 3,500 Polish troops (aided by 2,500

Jan Kiliński, shoemaker and rebel leader

Varsovian irregulars led by a butcher and a shoemaker) took on the 7,000 Russians. Despite having far better weapons and equipment, more than 50 per cent of the Russians were killed and most of the rest captured. Sadly, the uprising proved to be another of the incredibly heroic failures that characterise Polish history. In November 1794 Russian forces captured and pillaged the Praga district of Warsaw, murdering up to 20,000 civilians before burning the entire area. Eleven days later the Polish army surrendered and Poland disappeared from the map of the world for 123 years, its territory split between Russia, Prussia and Austria.

Hopes of independence were rekindled in 1806. The arrival of Napoleon Bonaparte in Poland coincided with the Greater Poland Uprising, and in 1807 Warsaw became the capital of the Duchy of Warsaw. The defeat of Napoleon's 1812 invasion of Russia led to Warsaw being captured yet again. After the 1815 Congress of Vienna, the Duchy of Warsaw became the Congress Kingdom of Poland, but that was very much a puppet state. On the plus side, Warsaw's university was established in 1816. Another rebellion in 1830, the November Uprising, saw Warsaw free itself, but it was captured once more in September 1831 after a series of battles in its suburbs. Protests against the Russian occupiers in 1861 ended with Russian troops firing into the crowd and killing five people. This

Marshal Józef Piłsudski, a Polish hero

was one of the factors that led to the formation of the Underground Polish National Government in Warsaw, a shadow government that commanded the January Uprising (1863–5). As with all previous rebellions, this failed and resulted in harsh action being taken by the Russian government: education in Polish was forbidden, Russian became the official language of the nation and up to 70,000 Poles were exiled to far-flung parts of Russia.

A modern city

In 1875 a senior Russian official finally realised that attempting to beat Varsovians into submission simply didn't work. Sokrates Starynkiewicz may have been a Russian general, but in the 17 years that he was Mayor of Warsaw the city flourished. All the trappings of a modern city appeared: the first railway bridge in 1875 (the first section of the Warsaw–Vienna railway had been started in 1845); the first telephone exchange in 1881; the first regular horse-drawn tram service in 1882 (the tram network was converted to electricity in 1907); the first modern sewage and water supply system (started in 1881, finished in 1898 and still in use today, and yes, you can drink the tap water here); both the gas system and street-lighting system were modernised and greatly expanded, and the first covered marketplace, Hala Mirowska (*see pp70–71*), was built.

While these years were good to Warsaw, Poland was still occupied by three separate countries. That changed after World War I, when Poland regained its independence in 1918 under the leadership of Józef Piłsudski. Over-ambitious ideas about where Poland's eastern border should be sparked the Polish–Soviet War in 1919, and by August 1920 Soviet forces were just 13km (8 miles) from Warsaw. However, they were stopped there in the decisive Battle of Warsaw. Opponents of Piłsudski ironically labelled this as the 'Miracle at the Vistula', but the name stuck. The battle marked the end of Soviet ambitions to start revolutions in the war-shattered nations of Europe and then invade those countries as part of Bolshevism's spread across the world.

The interwar years were good times for Warsaw. The city grew dramatically and by 1939 the population was 1.3 million, 70 per cent higher than in 1918. Entire districts (such as Żoliborz) had been built and the city greatly changed as part of the 'Europeanisation' programme of Mayor Stefan Starzyński. Several new parks were laid out, the city's first airport was opened, the vast majority of streets were given all-weather tarmac surfaces, and a tunnel opened under al. Jerozolimskie for trains to cross the heart of the city. Plans for an underground railway were drawn up, but Warsaw would need to wait another 60 years for its Metro to open. Known as the 'Paris of the East', the city was widely acknowledged as the best place to live in central and eastern Europe.

War-torn Warsaw

That all changed in five and a half years. The first German bombs fell on 1 September 1939 and the German army reached Warsaw on 8 September. The city surrendered on 21 September after 20 days of bitter, but hugely one-sided, fighting, which left 25,800 civilians and 6,000 Polish soldiers dead, and 10 per cent of the city destroyed. This was merely a taste of things to come; the Ghetto Uprising of 1943 (*see pp72–3*) and the Warsaw Uprising of 1944 (*see pp14–15*), along with German reactions to both, virtually wiped the city out. By the time the Red Army liberated Warsaw in January 1945, more than 85 per cent of the city had been destroyed, more than 700,000 Varsovians expelled from their city, and more than 550,000 killed, including virtually all of the 393,000 Jewish Varsovians.

The former Jewish ghetto immediately after World War II

The birth of Solidarity

It took three years to reconstruct enough buildings for the government to move back (from Łódź). Work continued until the 1970s, when an economic policy based on borrowing money abroad resulted in huge drops in the standard of living. By 1980 workers were desperate enough to call a general strike (despite bloodshed that followed similar strikes in 1956, 1958, 1970 and 1976); the first free trade union in the communist bloc, Solidarność, was born. In 1981 martial law was declared by a group of hard-liners, either to protect Poland from Soviet invasion or to protect their ill-gotten power (depending on whose version of history you believe), troops and tanks poured on to the streets and union leaders were thrown in prison. However, even putting military commissars in factories couldn't get the economy going, and by 1988 Solidarność was strong enough to again call a general strike. This led to the Round Table Talks of 1989 with a table 8.8m (29ft) in diameter (the joke at the time was that the world spitting record was 7.8m/26ft), and free elections later that year which saw Solidarność win more than 99 per cent of the seats not reserved for the Communist Party. The following year Lech Wałęsa became the first popularly elected president in Polish history and the first leader to be freely elected since 1926.

Poland in the 21st century

Poland joined the North Atlantic Treaty Organization (NATO) in 1999, but far wider changes came after 2004's accession to the European Union (EU). Up to 2 million Poles (more than 5 per cent of the population) left the country in search of a better life. However, massive foreign investment and several billion euros of EU funds, with the promise of much more to come, have had a very beneficial effect on the Polish economy. Selection as host for the Euro 2012 football championships has brought yet further investment and the city is now poised for a new golden age.

The Warsaw Uprising

No single event has had more impact on modern Warsaw than the uprising of 1944. For 63 days a group of Polish Home Army (Armia Krajowa, the AK) fighters, armed largely with home-made or captured weapons, held off a much larger and vastly better-equipped force composed of two Nazi battle groups. The plan was to liberate the city before the Soviet forces arrived. However, Joseph Stalin spotted an opportunity to wipe out many of the people who might oppose him after he took control of Poland: the Red Army reached the left bank of the Vistula River and then stopped its advance for 'technical reasons' until January 1945.

This is now the site of the Hotel Warsaw

Early successes saw much of the city liberated. For the first time in nearly five years the Polish flag flew publicly. The Polish post office reopened, printed stamps and started to organise deliveries. Newspapers without any censorship hit the streets. Warsaw was of very marginal strategic value and many German generals were opposed to attempting to recapture it. Adolf Hitler, however, ordered the uprising to be crushed with extreme prejudice, demanding that his forces kill all civilians and 'turn it [Warsaw] into a lake'.

In the first seven days of the uprising more than 40,000 civilians were murdered in the Wola district alone. SS Brigadeführer Reinefarth commented to a German army lieutenant, 'You see, this is our biggest problem. These refugees! I don't have enough ammunition to kill them all.' But Erich von dem Bach, the commander of the Warsaw operation from 7 August onwards, soon realised that such massacres only served to harden Varsovians' resolve and so ordered that they cease. However, atrocities continued throughout the uprising.

Stalin's refusal to order the Red Army to advance or to let the

Western Allies use airfields in the Ukraine meant that the only way to resupply the Home Army was long-range missions from captured air bases in southern Italy. Despite hundreds of such flights by the RAF and USAAF (planes were shot down by both the Germans and the Soviets), the supplies dropped would never be enough to hold off ever larger German forces. Home Army strongholds fell one by one until surrender documents were signed on 2 October 1944.

The statue of the Little Insurgent

After the surrender Nazi forces set about turning Warsaw into a lake, as Hitler had ordered. More than 45 per cent of Warsaw had been destroyed by 2 October 1944. After the 'Burning and Destruction Detachments' had finished, 85 per cent of the buildings were destroyed, and in many districts more than 95 per cent: a higher percentage than even Hiroshima suffered. Buildings of historical or political significance were particularly targeted. Some (such as Łazienki Palace and the church on pl. Zbawiciela) still have the holes that were drilled ready for explosives that were never detonated.

If you'd like to learn more about the 63 days that saw perhaps the most tragic event in Warsaw's history, visit the Warsaw Uprising Museum (*see below*). Located in a power station that used to supply electricity to all the trams in the city, it's arguably the best museum in Poland and essential viewing for any visitor to Warsaw. It is spread over three floors and organised largely chronologically, and all the displays have information in English. Allow at least two hours to go round. The uprising is also commemorated on pl. Krasińskich, where the first shots of the uprising were fired, by the monument erected in 1989 after the communist era ended. There are 500 stone tablets at various points in the city marking where Polish civilians were massacred and, perhaps most poignant of all, the statue of the Little Insurgent on ul. Podwale.

Warsaw Uprising Museum, ul. Przyokopowa 28. Open: Fri–Mon & Wed 10am–6pm, Thur 10am–8pm. Closed: Tue. Admission charge except on Sun.

Politics

Warsaw became an occasional residence of the local Duke in the early 13th century. The other four major cities in Poland had already celebrated their tricentenaries by then (Wroclaw in 1220, Kraków in 1266, Poznan in 1270 and Gdańsk in 1297). Yet Warsaw has outgrown them all, becoming capital of Poland in 1596, and dodging arrows, cannonballs, bullets and bombs ever since.

Consigning Czersk, the former capital of Mazovia, to provincial backwater status in 1413, Warsaw has risen from a castle with an attached village populated by fishermen to unquestionably the leading city in Poland. Home to the national parliament since 1569, the official city name alone tells you where you are: 'The Capital City of Warsaw'. Unfortunately, the city has been paying the price for that title for the last 400-odd years: it's been captured, pillaged and burnt by the Russians, Germans, Prussians, Swedes and Transylvanians; liberated by the French (somewhat embarrassingly); and, as a final insult, rebuilt under the instruction of the Soviets. Power supposedly corrupts, but in the case of Warsaw it has resulted in the city being invaded and/or destroyed every 50 years or so.

The political system of Poland is officially described as a bicameral representative democratic republic. It is unofficially described as bearing more than a passing resemblance to the Judean revolutionary groups in Monty Python's *Life of Brian*, a characteristic reflected in the old joke about ten Poles shipwrecked on a desert island forming twenty political parties within thirty days. Part of the reason for this is the hyper-proportional nature of the electoral system: any party that attracts more than 5 per cent of the vote enters parliament, thus making coalition government the norm rather than the exception and giving ample room for groups to split from existing parties.

The president of Poland is elected every five years and is limited to two terms. With an official residence on al. Krakowskie Przedmieście, the president is the head of state, supreme representative of Poland and commander-in-chief of the armed forces. The president represents Poland abroad, has the right (under certain circumstances) to dissolve parliament and, in theory, appoints the prime minister. However, the prime minister is in practice a politician who is able to command a majority in parliament.

The two chambers of the parliament, the *Sejm* (the lower house) and the *Senat* (the upper house), are elected every four years, or more often should the government so desire. Nonetheless, given the fact that at each of the four elections since 1993 not a single government has even got close to being re-elected, things have to get pretty bad before a coalition will split up, way past hatred or name-calling or wanting to have one's coalition partners imprisoned.

Both chambers meet in the buildings on ul. Wiejska, which were constructed as the home for the Polish parliament in 1947. As the parliament then was to have only one chamber, no provision was made for the *Senat*, and, after being elected in 1989, the two chambers shared the *Sejm*'s chamber before moving into the pavilion building where three former conference rooms were knocked into one amphitheatre.

Presidential Palace

Geography

Warsaw sits on both banks of the longest river in Poland, the Vistula. Most European cities are located on or beside a river, but only Warsaw has a wild river flowing through it. The Vistula is the last major wild river in Europe, and the city of Warsaw is split in two by it.

Warsaw owes its existence and status to the Vistula River, so it's not such a surprise that the river is pretty much allowed to do its own thing as it flows through the city. On the left bank there are some rather limited river walls but nothing like the scale found in places like London or Paris. Instead, there are small islands created on the slower right side of the river, and in summer they are often covered in rich, fresh green foliage. The Vistula seems quite content with this arrangement; it hasn't badly flooded the city in living memory.

Somewhat ironically, given that it was first developed because it was more defendable than Jazdów, Warsaw doesn't have a very favourable position strategically. However, the lack of defensive barriers means that there is nothing to stop the free flow of fresh air into the city. Compared to many other cities in Europe (and particularly in Poland), Warsaw has pretty clean air. The Vistula is recovering from decades

of pollution, and while swimming in the river is perhaps not the best of ideas, you can drink the tap water.

Warsaw is the only European city that has a national park inside its borders. The Kampinos National Park (*see pp138–9*), the second-largest national park in Europe, lies immediately next to the Bielany district on the northern edge of the city, and it is not unusual to see the occasional moose wandering around the suburbs. To the south of the city is the spa town of Konstancin-Jeziorna (*see p141*), a fashionable resort in the interwar years and still worth a visit when you've had enough of urbanised life. Some 31km (19 miles) to the northeast is Zegrzyński reservoir, the largest lake near Warsaw.

Warsaw's population is 1.7 million spread throughout the 517sq km (200 sq miles) that the city covers. Another 1.3 million live outside the city limits but within the Obszar Metropolitalny Warszawy, the Warsaw

Metropolitan Area. These figures make Warsaw the eighth-biggest city in the EU. Almost all of the tourist attractions are found in the city centre (Śródmieście district). Żoliborz is a quiet and rather charming neighbourhood to the north of the centre; Mokotów is its southern counterpart and home to Pole Mokotowskie park (*see pp98–9*). On the other side of the river two neighbourhoods offer an insight into what Warsaw used to be like: Saska Kępa (*see pp122–3*) is one of the more exclusive areas of Warsaw, while Praga (*see pp116–21*) is in the middle of a transformation from infamous crime hotspot to hyper-fashionable artsy neighbourhood, although the opinions of its inhabitants as to whether that is a good thing or not do vary somewhat.

Statue of the Syrena with Most Świętokrzyski behind her

Culture

Although Warsaw has had a lot of upheaval politically and militarily over the last five centuries with all the invasions and occupations, Varsovians have made significant contributions to European and global culture. Unfortunately, many of them had to leave their home city before they found success, but they left their mark and the city now offers a wealth of cultural experiences to both visitors and residents.

In the 18th century foreign artists were attracted to Warsaw because of the wealthy patrons they could find here. The years when Poland endured the partitions saw the trend reverse and many prominent talents emigrated. These included Fryderyk Chopin (1810–49), whose family lived for a time on Krakowskie Przedmieście, in the south wing of the Czapskich Palace. Chopin left for Paris aged 20, where the former child prodigy made his name as one of the best piano composers of all time.

Joseph Conrad (1857–1924), the celebrated author of novels that were often based on his experiences in the British merchant navy, was born Teodor Józef Konrad Nałęcz-Korzeniowski and lived on ul. Nowy Świat before emigrating to England in 1884 and eventually becoming a British citizen. Maria Skłodowska-Curie (1867–1934) was born in Warsaw's New Town (Nowe Miasto), and achieved international acclaim in Paris after moving there in her early twenties to study science. She became the first woman in France to obtain a doctorate, the first person to be twice awarded a Nobel Prize and the first female professor at the Sorbonne university. Poles tend to get very unhappy indeed when people call her Marie Curie.

Helena Modrzejewska (1840–1909) and Pola Negri (1896–1987) were both Polish actresses who made it big in the USA. Before she emigrated, Modrzejewska was very successful at Warsaw's variety theatre, Teatr Rozmaitości, and lived in the city for seven years. Negri was born Barbara Apolonia Chałupiec and trained as a ballet dancer before tuberculosis put a stop to her dancing career. She lived for a time on ul. Browarna before moving to Berlin and then to Hollywood, where she became a well-known silent film actress.

Before World War II Warsaw was home to a great many Jewish cultural figures. Isaac Bashevis Singer (1904–91) lived on ul. Krochmalna for years, working as a journalist before emigrating to the USA in 1935. It was there that he won his Nobel Prize for Literature, in 1978. The tenor Jan Kiepura started his singing career in the National Theatre in Warsaw before emigrating to the USA at the beginning of World War II with other prominent Jews. He is buried in Powązki Cemetery (*see p130*).

Another Polish cultural figure to have won worldwide acclaim was the poet and translator Czesław Miłosz (1911–2004). Putting an early diplomatic career behind him, Miłosz turned to writing and moved to the USA in 1960 to work as a professor at Berkeley. In 1980 he won the Nobel Prize for Literature.

Ignacy Jan Paderewski (1860–1941) and Arthur Rubinstein (1887–1982) are well-known musical Poles who lived and worked in Warsaw. The multi-talented Paderewski was a diplomat and politician as well as a composer and pianist. Not only did he lead the Philharmonic's first concert in 1901, he also became Poland's third prime minister in 1919. Following a stint as Polish ambassador to the League of Nations, he returned to his musical career. Rubinstein studied at the Warsaw Conservatoire before touring around Europe and the USA giving piano recitals. Living mainly in London

A concert at the National Philharmonic

during World War I and in the USA during World War II, Rubinstein finally retired aged 89.

One world-famous (infamous according to US prosecutors) Pole is Roman Polański (*b.* 1933). Although born in Paris, Polański was brought up in Poland before becoming famous as an Oscar-winning actor and director, best known for films like *Rosemary's Baby*, *Tess* and *The Pianist*. The last follows the tale of a Jewish piano player during the Nazi occupation of Warsaw in World War II. Another well-known name is Agnieszka Holland (*b.* 1948). She was born in Warsaw and worked for prominent film-makers Krzysztof Zanussi and Andrzej Wajda before making her own films. She emigrated to France in 1981, just before martial law was declared.

Cartouche at the entrance of an Old Town house

Cultural life in Warsaw continues to be vibrant. There are a number of highly regarded music festivals that mainly focus on celebrating Chopin's legacy. The Fryderyk Chopin International Piano Competition has been staged every five years since 1955, and is one of the world's oldest piano competitions, having been started in 1927. Winners of the competition are almost guaranteed a stellar musical career, and have the doors of the world's best concert halls opened to them. More regular Chopin piano concerts are put on free of charge throughout the summer, in the pleasant surroundings of the Royal Łazienki Park rose garden. These Sunday concerts take place at noon and 4pm under the statue of the great composer himself.

International jazz music is well represented in Warsaw, with regular musical events and festivals held in the city, particularly during the summer months. The Warsaw Summer Jazz Days has been running since 1992 and takes place in various venues across town. The Jazz Jamboree, which is one of the most important jazz festivals in Europe and is now run by the same man behind the Summer Jazz Days, has been part of the JVC Jazz Festival since 2002. It is usually held in the second half of October.

An annual Autumn Festival was started in 1956 to present new music from Poland and around the world; it's usually held in late September. Other

The Tomasz Stańko Quartet at the 2004 Tenth International Outdoor Jazz Festival in the Old Town

festivals include the Mozart Festival in June and July, which gives audiences the opportunity to hear all of Mozart's operas sung by the Warsaw Chamber Opera, and the Organ Music Festival, held in St John's Cathedral in July.

The National Opera and Warsaw Chamber Opera cater for opera lovers, with their varied repertoires. Classical music can be heard at the National Philharmonic concert halls, as well as at

a good number of palaces, churches and museums. Chamber music is regularly presented at the Royal Castle, Wilanów Palace and Royal Łazienki Park's Palace on the Water.

Culture in Warsaw may seem to be dominated by music, but this is not its only focus. Theatre and dance are performed in many venues, and museums covering almost every subject imaginable are also on offer (*see pp124–7 & 146–7*).

Warsaw legends

Warsaw has a rich selection of myths and legends. Among the characters that pop up most frequently are a mermaid with a great voice and a dragon undone by a shield of mirrors.

The Syrena

Back when the seas were unpolluted enough to support them, two mermaid sisters left the Atlantic and

The Syrena with her sword and shield

headed into the Baltic. The younger of the two decided Copenhagen would be a good home. She's still there today and her statue graces Copenhagen harbour. The older sister headed to the Polish coast and then decided to swim up the Vistula River. When she reached Warsaw she realised it was a good place to live and made her home on the sandy banks of the river, from where she sang beautiful songs every evening. She developed the habit of cutting fishermen's nets with her sword, but the nightly concerts were so wonderful that the locals decided it was a price worth paying. That is, all except an overzealous priest who could not accept her singing on Sundays. He pestered the fishermen until enough of them were willing to help him capture the mermaid and stop her ungodly song. However, the priest made the mistake of leaving his prize catch alone with an impressionable young man who found the voice and beauty of the Syrena (by now she'd started spelling her name the Polish way) so spectacular that he released her into the river. From then on there were no more riverside concerts but the Syrena promised to help the people of Warsaw whenever they needed protection. Varsovians always portray her holding a sword and a shield, but she's never been seen using either in any of the uprisings or during the times the city needed defending.

The Bazyliszek

The dragon in Kraków is more famous and supposedly far bigger, but Warsaw's dragon is like the city: unique, underrated and impossible to kill. The Old Town was once home to the Bazyliszek – a monster with a red-crested head, long serpentine neck, hairy legs and a body covered with black feathers. It was supposedly hatched from an egg laid by a seven-year-old rooster and incubated by a poisonous snake. Its stare turned humans to stone and the beast lived underground, warning people away with otherworldly howls. But it takes more than a funny glance and weird noises to strike fear into Varsovian hearts, especially when a rumour goes around that the dragon sleeps on a hoard of gold. Various thieves and barbarians ventured in search of it and never returned, but that was of no concern to the people of Warsaw; it just made the city a better place.

One day three over-bold children decided to steal the dragon's gold. One of them, Waluś, the ten-year-old son of a poor widow, fell victim to a

A reminder of the Bazyliszek

deadly glare from the creature, and his two friends, Maciek and Halszka, were trapped in a cellar by the beast. Eventually, a volunteer with a working knowledge of Greek mythology was found and issued with the equipment he requested: a shield made of mirrors and several heroic draughts of vodka. Suitably emboldened, our hero crept around the cellars until he lured the Bazyliszek into staring at the mirror. It gave an unearthly shriek of 'I woulda got away with it if it wasn't for you meddling kids!' and vanished. One of the few traces of the Bazyliszek to be found in Warsaw is an Old Town restaurant that bears its name and a metal statue of the beast outside.

Impressions

Warsaw has been making a considerable effort to improve its image. Facilities for visitors are now much better than they were ten years ago and the city is a far more welcoming place. With great dollops of cash being liberally spread around as the city gets ready to host football's Euro 2012, things are set to get even better.

When to go

Winter can start as early as 1 October and finish as late as 30 April. January has an average minimum temperature of −17°C (1°F), February −16°C (3°F), but −30°C (−22°F) is not unheard of in either month. That's too cold for much sightseeing. Snow is quickly cleared from roads but slowly (if at all) from pavements, and walking on sheets of ice is unpleasantly common. Spring usually arrives in April, and that month, May and June are ideal times to visit: the city awakes from a long cold winter and comes back to life. July and August see the mercury rise above 30°C (85°F), not oppressively hot but warm enough to make air conditioning a pleasant luxury. Varsovians tend to get out of town during summer, especially at weekends, which can leave the city somewhat deserted. Summer is the wettest time of the year but relative humidity is still low, making the heat no worse than moderately uncomfortable, and every other day is completely without rainfall. By September things are beginning to cool off but autumn can be the best time to visit: the season's rich hues coincide with a rich time for cultural events. In November temperatures are once again uncomfortably cold.

Getting there and around

Warsaw is the hub of the nation's road and rail networks, making every border crossing easy to reach. The main train station, Warszawa Centralna (Warsaw Central), is located in the centre and served by the vast majority of long-distance trains to the capital. Some trains only go as far as Warszawa Wschodnia (Warsaw East) in the Praga district and a few only to Warszawa Zachodnia (Warsaw West) in Wola. Care is recommended at both those stations, particularly at night, although Warsaw Central Station is not a place you would want to hang around in the evenings either. Most visitors arrive by air. The airport (Warsaw Fryderyk Chopin airport) is located 10km (6¼ miles) to the southeast of the city centre (*see pp174–5*).

Repeatedly being destroyed and reconstructed has left Warsaw without a single central area. The city is not well suited to getting around on foot, although most of the individual neighbourhoods can be explored that way. In the Old Town (Stare Miasto) and the New Town (Nowe Miasto) there is no other choice because both are entirely pedestrianised. Many Varsovians bemoan the lack of more than a single underground Metro line, but most visitors find that the trams

and buses provide very acceptable transport. In rush hours the tram is a far better choice than the bus: Warsaw has few bus lanes and those that exist are often used by unauthorised vehicles. There are two bus routes aimed at tourists: bus No 180 (*see pp64–5*) and bus No 100 (runs only at weekends). Taxis are relatively inexpensive and often reasonably honest. For more details on public transport including taxis, *see pp183–6*.

Navigation
The Palace of Culture and Science is visible for 20km (12½ miles) in any direction, which makes it a good

The tram network offers a convenient way of getting from A to B

The Palace of Culture and Science

reckoning point. Combine it with the Marriott Hotel and the InterContinental Hotel and you should be able to work out where you are pretty much anywhere inside the city limits. While the river is not embraced by the city, it does play an important role in navigation: for east–west streets, house numbers rise as you move away from the river; for north–south streets, house numbers rise as you move north. Almost every building now has a large sign giving its number, street name (*ulica* or ul. means street; *aleje* or al. means avenue) and the neighbourhood. Certain pre-war streets now have a less than logical route: ul. Piękna enters pl. Konstytucji then disappears for 200m (220yds); ul. Chmielna vanishes from the city centre under both the Palace of Culture and Science and Zlote Tarasy before reappearing in the Wola district.

Safety

Despite appearances to the contrary, Warsaw is a reasonably safe city by European standards. That said, late-night robbery is by no means unheard of and pickpocketing is far more common, so keep your valuables out of sight and well secured. There have been several cases in recent years of foreigners being given vodka spiked with drugs; all were robbed and at least two died. Being drunk in public can result in the police taking you for an overnight stay in the 'drunk-tank', with no access to lawyers or telephones, so exercise caution when you go out and don't drink to excess.

Warsaw environs

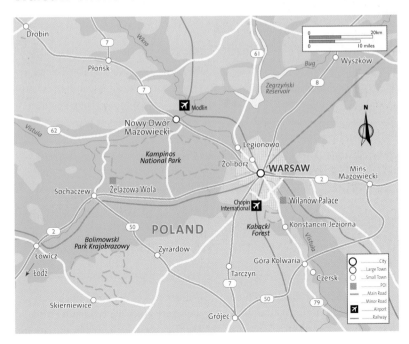

The Palace of Culture and Science

The palace as seen from ul. Świętokrzyska

If there is one thing Varsovians hold wildly differing views about, it is the Palace of Culture and Science (Pałac Kultury i Nauki, PKiN for short). Some regard it as a hideous monstrosity that Stalin left as an unwelcome gift in the 1950s, but others see it as a strangely beautiful relic and a reminder to Poles of their historic ties with Russia. Whatever your opinion, there is no denying the sheer size of this building.

The structure was built from more than 40 million bricks. Surprisingly, it is only 30 storeys in total, but each floor is unusually high, and, at over 230m (755ft), this is the tallest building in Poland. The clock, which was added for the Millennium, was the highest timepiece in the world at its installation, but has since been overtaken by a clock tower in Tokyo. It is, however, still the tallest four-faced clock tower in the world.

The architecture of the palace is similar to Soviet skyscrapers erected at around the same time, but the architect, Lev Rudnev, did travel around Poland to try to bring in Polish influences. Some of the masonry is reminiscent of that used in Kraków's Renaissance buildings.

Although largely made up of office space, the palace also boasts cafés, theatres, shops, cinema screens and conference facilities spread around its 3,288 rooms. Temporary exhibitions are held fairly regularly in the grand marble-lined rooms of the first floor, and big international expos are also drawn to the grand venue. The scientific attractions include the rather dusty technology museum and the child-friendly evolution museum, while the plays and films on offer, as well as nightclubs 1955 and Quo Vadis, are just some of the cultural attractions the palace provides. The 'Youth palace' section of the building contains a swimming pool, gyms and a winter garden. Children can get involved in all kinds of activities here, from language lessons to sports tournaments, and during the summer months there are often groups of young people bouncing balls on the basketball courts by the entrance. In winter the courts are turned into an ice rink.

The Congress Hall (Sala Kongresowa), formerly the venue for Communist Party congresses, now hosts festivals, concerts and other events. Big names that have performed here include Louis Armstrong, Marlene Dietrich and Leonard Cohen. The Rolling Stones played here in 1967, their first concert behind the Iron Curtain. The palace's theatres include the Theatre of Dramatic Art (Teatr Dramatyczny), the Studio Theatre (Teatr Studio) and the Puppet Theatre (Teatr Lalka).

One of the palace's biggest tourist draws, the viewing terrace on the 30th floor, provides a reasonable view of the city. It is unfortunately just a touch too far from areas like the Old and New Towns to provide a truly satisfying vantage point, but it gives visitors a general picture of how Warsaw fits together.

The outside of the building at ground level is decorated with over-sized social-realist statues and fountains. It is worth walking around if not all then at least part of the outside, just to inspect the proud expressions on the statues' faces and appreciate the enormity of the construction. City authorities are constantly announcing plans to revamp the area surrounding the palace. With any luck one of these plans will come to fruition some day soon: already the ugly parking area with its supermarket and covered market are a thing of the past. Such a majestic building deserves a more dignified setting.

Decorative stonework on the lower sections

The Old Town

The Stare Miasto (Old Town) was first built in the late 13th and early 14th centuries as housing for the court of the Dukes of Mazovia and the people who served them. It is the oldest part of Warsaw and still retains its medieval street plan. Devastated during World War II, it has since been restored to breathtaking beauty. This amazing restoration has won the area a well-deserved place on the list of UNESCO World Heritage sites.

The area began to develop into its current form from 1569 when Warsaw became the meeting place for the Grand *Sejm* (the parliament) of the Polish-Lithuanian Commonwealth. By 1596 Warsaw had also become the site of the official residence of the king of Poland. Soon the patricians of the city wanted imposing residences of their own. To go with a palace in what was then the countryside near the town, men of real status also needed a town house, preferably one of the houses that had sprung up around the Rynek (the Market Square). As times, fortunes and tastes changed, these patricians were replaced by newly rich politicians, business people and artists. As the heart of the city moved slowly southwards, the area became mainly inhabited by the lower classes and fell into disrepair. When Poland regained independence in 1918, the Royal Castle became the seat of the president of Poland and work started on restoring the Old Town. This work had largely been completed by

1939, only for the Luftwaffe to destroy a considerable number of buildings during the air raids aimed specifically at civilian targets.

Sgraffito on an Old Town house

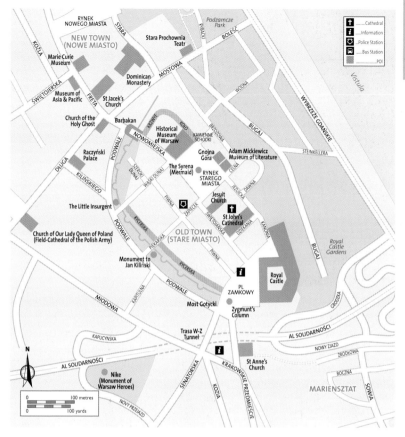

Some of the most bitter fighting of the Warsaw Uprising (*see pp14–15*) took place in the Old Town in August 1944. Thick medieval walls that had stood for 400 years offered no protection against German tanks and artillery. Neither did the churches and cathedrals: St John's Cathedral suffered several attacks by German 'Goliath' self-propelled mines (*see p40*), and churches being used by the insurgents as hospitals were bombed repeatedly. After the capitulation of the Home Army (Armia Krajowa), Nazi demolition teams flattened the buildings that still stood.

Zygmunt's Column

The ideal starting point for a tour around the Old Town is the column of King Zygmunt III (the king who moved the royal court to Warsaw from Kraków), which stands in the centre of pl. Zamkowy. Dating from 1643, it is the oldest secular monument in Warsaw; the only older one in Poland is the statue of Neptune in Gdańsk's main and destroyed by the Nazis in World War II. Two of the three columns can be seen lying on the lawn between the Royal Castle and the steps down to al. Solidarności; touching them is supposed to bring luck. The statue was badly damaged in World War II, losing both its sabre and a hand. Restoring the king to the top of his column was part of the restoration of the Old Town, and since 1949 Zygmunt has once again been watching over his city, albeit now 6m (20ft) away from his original position.

Town houses on the corner of pl. Zamkowy

square. As well as the large cross in his left hand, the king carries a sabre in his right hand. Legend has it that Zygmunt would often raise his sabre to inspire his troops before battle and that the statue still raises its sabre to warn Varsovians every time the city is in danger.

Before the 22m (72ft) high monument was built by Zygmunt III's son, King Władysław IV, only statues of saints had been displayed atop such columns in northern Europe. Designed by Italian-born architect Konstanty Tencalli and sculptor Clemente Molli, the statue was cast in bronze by Daniel Tym and currently stands on a Corinthian-style column made of granite, the fourth column the statue has had. The first two columns were both made of marble, the first Polish and the second pink Italian marble. The third was made of granite, installed in 1826

Plac Zamkowy (Castle Square)

Construction of pl. Zamkowy as it currently stands was finished in 1818, and it is dominated by the Royal Castle (*see pp44–5*). The southern end of the square marks the start of ul. Krakowskie Przedmieście, arguably the grandest and most beautiful street in Warsaw. Particularly worth a couple of minutes is the town house of the Prazmowski family at No 87. Built in the mid-17th

TRASA W-Z TUNNEL

Next door to Literacka at 1/3 pl. Zamkowy is the top of escalators that go down to the Trasa W-Z Tunnel underneath pl. Zamkowy. The tunnel was built in 1947–9 as part of the post-war reconstruction and hugely improved traffic flow in the city, although it came close to destroying St Anne's Church (*see pp82–3*). The escalators were the first in Warsaw and opened to great fanfare in 1949. After being closed for nearly a decade, they were renovated and reopened to the public on 21 July 2005. Don't miss the wonderful socialist-realist statues at the bottom end.

century for the royal physician, it was extensively remodelled in 1754, hence its more modern appearance. The building is now owned by the Writers' Association of Poland and is home to a rather pleasant café named Literacka, which is an ideal spot to enjoy a coffee and the view of pl. Zamkowy.

Most Gotycki (The Gothic Bridge)

Duke Janusz I Siemowitowic gave Warsaw permission to erect city walls in 1379 and an exemption from taxes for eight years to help cover the cost of those walls. The remainder of the old Brama Krakowska (Kraków Gate) is long gone but the bridge to it still remains. Built in the late 15th century, the bridge crossed the moat that ran in front of the old city walls. After being partially demolished in 1808 and then forgotten about, it was uncovered in 1977 during the reconstruction of the Royal Castle, restored and reopened to pedestrians in 1983.

Ulica Świętojańska (St John's Street)

Running from pl. Zamkowy to the Rynek (the Market Square), ul. Świętojańska was once the most important street in Warsaw and is dominated by St John's Cathedral and the Jesuit Church (*see p40*). Devastated during World War II, the façades of the houses were rebuilt using many of the 16th-century door and window frames that had been salvaged from the rubble of the Old

Jesuit Church and St John's Cathedral

Horse-drawn carriage tours: the best way to sightsee in the Old Town

Town. The Mansjonaria house at No 2, originally built in the late 15th century, has a particularly interesting blend of Renaissance and Gothic styling, the result of its reconstruction in 1688 by Italian architects Antonio Visconti and Bernardo Morando. No 11 bears the Warsaw coat of arms and a statue called *The Warsaw Townswoman*. No 31 is called Pod Okrętem (Under the Ship) and sports a plaster relief above its door showing one of the sailing ships that made the house's owner his money. Świętojańska is one of Warsaw's narrowest streets and usually the most crowded in the city.

Ulica Piwna (Beer Street)

Although it runs parallel to the crowded Świętojańska just a few metres away, ul. Piwna is a much quieter street and well deserving of a place on the route of any stroll around the Old Town. Sadly, the former homes of well-off freemen were not restored with as much authentic detail as Świętojańska, and the façades are now mainly pseudo-antique. One façade that proudly shows a modern element is on the house at No 6, Pod Gołębiami (Under the Pigeons), which features a relief showing pigeons. Installed in 1953, it is in honour of a woman who lived in the ruins of the house after its destruction in 1944 so that she could take care of the pigeons of the Old Town. Another bird is found above the door of the house at No 18. This one is an eagle and marks the house of the Crown Metricants: document keepers who worked in the royal archives and courts, the forerunners of what we now know as bureaucrats.

Ulica Piekarska (Baker Street)

Halfway down ul. Piwna you'll find ul. Piekarska running southwest to ul. Podwale. Once it had timber houses that were home to the millers and bakers of the city, but those were long ago replaced by stone houses. The corner of ul. Piekarska and ul. Rycerska used to have a small square called Piekiełko (the Inferno) where witches were burnt at the stake during the 16th and 17th centuries. It's also where the unsuccessful assassin of King Zygmunt III, Michał Piekarski, was executed. One of the most interesting houses on ul. Piekarska is No 4, Pod Pawiem (Under the Peacock). Designed by Antonio Fontana and built in the 1750s, the reconstruction work (from 1959 to 1961) managed to save much of the original façade. At the corner of ul.

The Barbican, now restored to its 16th-century form

Piekarska and ul. Podwale stands a **monument to Jan Kiliński**, a shoemaker who became one of the leaders of the Varsovian civilian army during the Kościuszko Uprising. Made in 1935, this is now the third home for the statue: it initially stood in pl. Krasiński but was damaged by the Nazis and moved to al. 3 Maja before being placed at its current location in 1959.

The Little Insurgent

Turn right at Kiliński's monument (corner of ul. Piekarska and ul. Podwale), walk along the city walls and you'll come to a statue that tugs a little on the heartstrings: the Little Insurgent. This statue commemorates the child soldiers who fought in the Warsaw Uprising and shows a boy wearing a helmet that is far too large for him and carrying a sub-machine-gun. The insurgent on whom the statue is modelled was a 13-year-old named Antek who was killed on 8 August 1944.

Barbakan (The Barbican)

Further on around the city walls is the Barbakan. During the 16th century the old city walls, made of earth and dating from the founding of Warsaw, were replaced with brick walls. These had only two gates: Brama Krakowska (Kraków Gate) to the south (*see p35*) and Brama Nowomiejska (New Town Gate) to the north. The Barbakan was built in 1548 to protect the New Town (Nowe Miasto) gate. Designed by

Venetian architect Giovanni Battista, it features four defensive towers and a bridge over the moat. Partially demolished in the 17th century, it was rebuilt in the early 19th century before being abandoned. After being excavated and almost entirely restored between 1936 and 1939, it was destroyed in World War II. What you can see now is a result of a reconstruction between 1946 and 1954 and is based on the Barbican of the late 16th century. In recent years the Barbican has become a place for artists to sell somewhat overpriced small paintings and wooden statuettes. Just outside the Barbican an executioner can usually be found waving a (blunt) axe at passers-by and staging mock executions, for the right price of course.

Wąski Dunaj and Szeroki Dunaj

The name 'Dunaj' is taken from the stream that runs away from the charming little square called Szeroki Dunaj (the Wide Dunaj), which is usually far quieter than the often crowded Rynek (Market Square). This part of town retains the street plan laid out in the 14th century with the houses dating from 1478, the year of a fire that destroyed much of the area. The

Houses on Szeroki Dunaj

The Syrena stands guard in the Old Town Rynek (Market Square)

original home of the city's Jewish community, Szeroki Dunaj was the site of a fish and meat market during the 17th century and later both a vegetable market and a flower market. The centre of the square has a 20th-century well that was installed in 1970, a replacement for the 17th-century well destroyed during World War II. The two most interesting houses on the square are both linked to tradesmen: Przy Bramie Rzeźniczej (By the Butcher's Gate), which stands next to Brama Rzeźnicza (the Butcher's Gate), and the house at No 10 Szeroki Dunaj, which was the original home of the guild of shoemakers. No 5 was once home to a famous Varsovian shoemaker, Jan Kiliński, of Kościuszko Uprising fame. Most of the houses in the square are decorated with superb sgraffito; although it is not original, having been added during the reconstruction of the area, it is some of the finest in the city.

Wąski Dunaj (the Narrow Dunaj) runs from Szeroki Dunaj to the Rynek and has some fine sgraffito. The house at No 11, Pod Chrystusem (Under Christ), takes its name from a statue of Christ dating from the mid-18th century, but sadly the statue was removed during the communist era.

Walk: Old Town

Start on ul. Świętojańska, at the end near pl. Zamkowy, and walk towards the Old Town Rynek (Market Square), making sure to stop off at St John's Cathedral on the way (No 8), and the Jesuit Church next door. Visit the Historical Museum of Warsaw in the Rynek. From there, walk to Kamienne Schodki, take in the views from Gnojna Góra, then head for ul. Kanonia.

Allow about 3 hours.

1 St John's Cathedral

Looming over the town houses that line ul. Świętojańska is St John's Cathedral, whose presence can be dated back to the 14th century. Over the years it was remodelled and decoration added; however, post-war architects decided to rebuild it as close to the original form as possible. St John's is notable as the site of numerous coronations, while its crypts hold the remains of Stanisław Augustus Poniatowski (Poland's last monarch), President Gabriel Narutowicz and literary hero Henryk Sienkiewicz. The cathedral suffered extensive damage during the Warsaw Uprising and today a rusty tank-track, recovered from a German self-propelled mine detonated inside the cathedral, can be found adorning an exterior wall.
Go next door to the Jesuit Church at ul. Świętojańska 10.

2 Jesuit Church

Next door to the cathedral is Warsaw's Jesuit Church, founded in the early 17th century by Piotr Skarga, confidant and confessor of King Zygmunt III. The 65m (213ft) steeple remains one of the lasting memories of Warsaw's skyline, and though the church has in turn been ransacked and destroyed by both Swedes and Germans, it is still very much of public interest. Elements that survived Nazi destruction include a picture of the Holy Mother of Grace, revered for its miracle-working properties.
Continue along ul. Świętojańska to the Rynek and visit the Historical Museum of Warsaw at Rynek Starego Miasta 28/42.

3 Historical Museum of Warsaw

This is a vast museum whose route carries visitors up winding staircases and through 60 rooms that are closely guarded by ladies quite possibly older than the relics they keep safe from hideous fates (such as being breathed on). The tour begins with a short black-and-white film showing the city in ruins in 1944 and then starts in earnest with

Colourful façades characteristic of the Old Town

archaeological finds dating back to the city's early beginnings. From there it's an odyssey through the life and times of Warsaw, with visitors treated to a staggering range of historical objects.

From here, follow the square round to Kamienne Schodki.

4 Kamienne Schodki (Stone Stairs)

Take a walk down the narrow set of stairs that connects the Old Town's Rynek with ul. Brzozowa. Locals claim Napoleon savoured the view in 1812 while contemplating his impending march on Moscow.

At the bottom of the stairs, turn right and continue on to Gnojna Góra.

5 Gnojna Góra (Dung Hill)

The area between ul. Brzozowa and Celna is commonly known as Gnojna

Góra (Dung Hill), a hint at the site's medieval incarnation as the town dump. Today it has a viewing platform that offers a panorama of the Vistula River, as well as a beer garden to reward the dutiful sightseer.

Head back towards the Rynek by dipping under the arched buildings on ul. Dawna – arguably the Old Town's most attractive street. Turn left at the end.

6 Ulica Kanonia

Finish your tour of the Old Town on the square in ul. Kanonia. The church bell that sits in the middle of the diminutive square was recovered from the rubble of St John's Cathedral, while the white overhead walkway linking the cathedral to the castle was specifically constructed following a botched assassination attempt on King Zygmunt III.

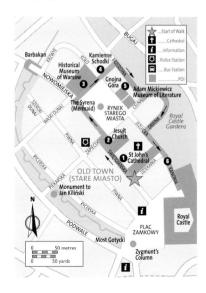

The Old Town Market Square

The Rynek Starego Miasta (Old Town Market Square) dates back to the very earliest days of Warsaw. At just 90m by 73m (295ft by 240ft), it is one of the smaller market squares in Poland but also one of the most beautiful in Europe. It has hosted a variety of events, from markets to executions, and from 1429 to 1817 it housed the wooden building that was Warsaw's first city hall. On 2 December 1789 the leading freemen of the city, led by their mayor and all dressed in black, walked from the Rynek to the Royal Castle to petition the king and the parliament with a list of reforms. This act led to Europe's first modern constitution: the Constitution of 3 May 1791.

The four sides of the Rynek are named after four famous Varsovians who once lived in the houses of the market square. The northern side takes its name from Jan Dekert, the mayor of Warsaw who led the freemen in 1789. Its houses date from the 16th to the 18th century and it has two particularly interesting buildings: the Baryczkowska residence (No 32), the best-preserved building on the Rynek and the only one in the Old Town that has an original 18th-century attic; and the Falkiewicz residence (No 28), with its top floor decorated on both sides with carvings of the Virgin Mary, St Stanislaus and St Elizabeth.

Named after lawyer Franciszek Barss, the eastern side was completely destroyed during World War II. It has since been rebuilt using many old elements; most notably, the house at No 20 has an original Gothic doorway and a reconstructed Gothic vestibule and is now the home of the Adam Mickiewicz Museum of Literature. No 6 is the 15th-century Giza family residence with a rather fine 17th-century doorway. The façade of the Orlemusowska family residence (No 22) is one of the most beautiful in the Old Town and features a Baroque doorway. The entire side has dormer windows to provide light to the stairwells.

The first mayor of Warsaw, Ignacy Zakrzewski-Wyssogota, gives his name to the southern side of the Rynek. Although not original, many of the façades are from the late 18th and early 19th centuries. Among the original details are the Renaissance-style doorway on the house at No 1 and the Renaissance gable on the house at No 13, Pod Lwem (Under the Lions), which still bears its plaster relief of lions. Also of note are the Bazyliszek restaurant at No 5, Pod Bazyliszkiem (Under the Basilisk), one-time home of Warsaw's dragon (*see p25*), and the sundial on the wall which the house at No 1 shares with ul. Świętojańska.

The western side is named after statesman and scholar Hugo Kołłątaj and has façades with a mixture of 18th-century and Gothic details as well as a clock designed by Jerzy Brabander and Zygmunt Kropisz. The town house at No 27 dates from the 15th century and is known as the Fukier house. Originally owned by the Korba family, who used it to run a winery famed for its *miód pitny* (mead), the Fukier family purchased the property in 1810 and continued the business. Now home to the U Fukiera restaurant run by Magda Gessler, one of the best restaurants in the city (*see p161*), it features a wonderful restored cloistered courtyard (originally designed by Władysław Marconi) and excellent cellars.

The Dekert side of the Old Town Rynek, home to the Historical Museum of Warsaw

The Royal Castle

Despite looking several hundred years old, the Royal Castle is only just old enough to buy alcohol. After standing for some 650 years, it was razed to the ground by the Nazis in World War II. Reconstruction work started in 1971, but the scale of the project was so huge that it took 17 years to complete.

There has been a fortified residence on this site since 1282. At first it was an occasional residence of the Duke of Mazovia, but when he moved to Warsaw permanently in 1413, the castle became far more substantial. After 1569, when the Polish-Lithuanian parliament chose Warsaw to be its home and the place where the kings of Poland would be elected, development of the castle grew markedly. However,

The clock tower crowns the Royal Castle

RESTORATION

After the significant damage caused by bombing and Nazi arson in 1939, the curators of the Royal Castle managed to smuggle out a considerable number of paintings, and some of the furniture, carvings, woodwork and wainscoting, before the majority of the building was dynamited in late 1944. To supplement these original features, suitable period works were donated from all corners of the world, enabling the Royal Castle to reopen in 1988. The results of the restoration were so successful that the castle has been placed on the UNESCO World Heritage List with the rest of the Old Town.

King Zygmunt III's decision to move the royal court to Warsaw meant a much larger building was needed.

Three Italian architects, Giovanni Trevano, Giacomo Rodondo and Matteo Castelli, started work in 1598 and completed their project in 1619. Among the buildings added to the original castle were the Grand Court, the Small Court, the Grodzka Tower and the New House of Zygmunt II. Subsequent centuries saw the castle extended several times. On the orders of King Władysław IV, a terrace overlooking the garden was added and the Władysławowska Tower was built in 1637–43. In the 18th century, during the reign of Augustus III, two new wings were added: the rococo-style Wettin wing facing the Vistula River (built 1737–46), and the northern wing called the 'Yard'.

King Stanisław Augustus Poniatowski ordered the construction of the Royal

Apartments on the first floor of the castle. These apartments now contain the Canaletto Room. Despite the name, this room actually contains paintings of 18th-century Warsaw that were done not by Giovanni Antonio Canal (to give Canaletto his full name) but by his nephew, Bernardo Bellotto (who sometimes signed his work Bernardo Canaletto). Near the Canaletto Room is the Royal Chapel, built in 1776. The chapel is the resting place of the urn containing the ashes of national hero Tadeusz Kościuszko. Also dating from the time of Augustus Poniatowski is the stunning Marble Room where the king held 'Thursday Dinners' with leading figures of the Polish enlightenment. Portraits of several Polish kings, painted by Marcello Bacciarelli and Jan Bogumił Plersch, are hung in the room. The same king commissioned the Royal Library, built to a design by Domenico Merlini. The rooms of the library, designed by Wilhelm Henryk Minter in 1814, are the only completely original interiors in the castle today.

Opening times vary in the different parts of the castle. No phone number is given as there is rarely an English speaker available to give information.

The lavishly decorated Marble Room, scene of the King Augustus Poniatowski's 'Thursday dinners'

The New Town

Just like the Old Town (Stare Miasto), Warsaw's New Town (Nowe Miasto) is a magnet for tourists and visited regularly by most Varsovians. The New Town was also reconstructed from the ground up after World War II, but it has an atmosphere and charm quite distinct from the more crowded Old Town.

The New Town developed outside the city walls; in fact, it never had any real defensive walls. It grew up from the 15th century onwards and was home to craftspeople and artisans. As these people were lower down the economic food chain than the traders and courtiers who made their home in the Old Town, the New Town was built with fewer 'grand' buildings and less ostentatiousness. However, the unplanned nature of the area made for wider streets and more light and space than the Old Town offers.

The logical place to start a trip around the New Town is the Barbakan (Barbican). Directly in front of you is the charming ul. Freta, and just a few steps along it, to your right, is ul. Mostowa.

Ulica Mostowa (Bridge Street)

Once little more than a track leading down a gorge in the Vistula scarp to a ford across the river, ul. Mostowa gained importance and its very name when Warsaw's first permanent bridge across the Vistula was completed in 1573. Becoming an important transport link gave the street status, reflected in the fact that it was paved as early as 1595, one of the first streets outside the Old Town to receive such luxury. The street became home to a varied collection of craftspeople and traders and built up a reputation for its fine eating establishments and dubious drinking dens. Sadly, all trace of those is now long gone. The street was flattened in World War II and rebuilt between 1948 and 1956 to a less than authentic design. However, a few well-placed classical touches don't do many streets much harm and Mostowa is no exception, especially the house at No 9 with its wonderful sgraffito and mosaics.

Stara Prochownia Teatr (Old Gunpowder Store Theatre)

Originally built in 1581, this building has had a varied history. At first it was

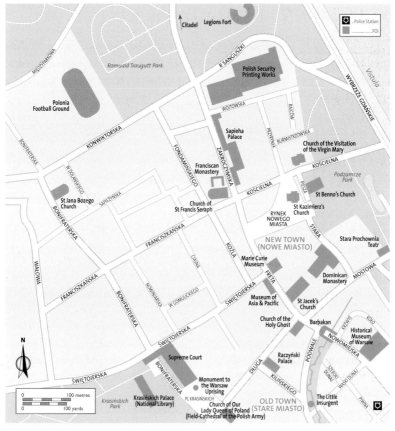

Bridge Gate and protected the bridge (*see opposite*). Then in 1646 it was remodelled so it could serve as a place for the city to store its gunpowder. Following the Kościuszko Uprising, it was converted into a prison to lock up the sudden surplus of rebels the city had acquired. After they had all seen the error of their ways, the prison was converted into a residential building. That was destroyed during the Warsaw Uprising and then 17 years later rebuilt as the Stara Prochownia

Teatr (the Old Gunpowder Store Theatre), opening in 1965.

Church of the Holy Ghost

Back up ul. Mostowa to ul. Freta and almost directly opposite you, slightly to your right, is the Church of the Holy Ghost at ul. Nowomiejska 23. The original 14th-century church, built from wood along with the hospital next to it, was burnt down when the Swedish army captured Warsaw in 1655. The Baroque replacement that can be seen today was begun in 1707 and completed in 1711. Since that date the church has been the starting point for Varsovians making the annual pilgrimage to Częstochowa, Poland's spiritual capital. Although destroyed in 1944, the church was rebuilt in virtually identical form in the 1950s. Also rebuilt then was the smallest house in Warsaw (at Długa 1). Originally built at the end of the 18th century on the smallest plot of land in the city, the house is sadly no longer inhabited; instead, it has been converted into a newspaper kiosk. *ul. Nowomiejska 23.*

Rynek Nowego Miasta (The New Town Market Square)

Unlike the Old Town's Rynek, which is almost a perfect square, the New Town's Rynek is these days rather closer to a triangle. Fortunately, the unplanned development that led to this has only added to the charm of the place, and it is still far larger and infinitely less crowded than its Old Town neighbour. First laid out in 1408 when the New Town was founded, the Rynek was then rectangular and from 1680 to 1818 it contained the New Town's town hall. The New Town was then a separate entity from the Old Town and even had its own coat of arms, featuring a unicorn and a virgin, which can be seen on ironwork of the 19th-century well situated in the square close to ul. Freta. The area around the square was the scene of fighting, which was bitter even by the standards of the Warsaw

Uprising, and all of the buildings suffered extensive damage. The reconstruction programme started in 1949 when it was decided to build the Nowe Miasto, preserving the original medieval street plan but replacing most of the buildings with new structures not designed to look like their predecessors. Construction started in 1952 and was completed in 1957. While the results are less than authentic, they are rather pleasant and well worth spending some time checking out.

St Kazimierz's Church

Standing on the eastern side of the New Town Rynek is the complex that contains St Kazimierz's Church and the convent of the Benedictines of the Perpetual Adoration of the Blessed Sacrament. The church was built in 1688 at the order of Queen Maria Sobieska to honour the victory of her husband, King Jan III Sobieski, over the Turkish army outside Vienna. The design is by Tylman van Gameren and features several Palladian-style elements, particularly the dome. Designs inspired by the Italian architect Andrea Palladio were often used during the reconstruction work that followed the three occasions when Warsaw was captured and pillaged between 1655 and 1658. Sadly, very few of those buildings survive today. St Kazimierz's suffered particularly badly during the Warsaw Uprising: while it was being used as a hospital by the Home Army it received a direct hit from a German bomb and more than 1,000 civilians were killed. The reconstruction of the church took six years (1949–55) and made use of highly detailed measurements that had been taken in 1925 and 1933. Unfortunately, most of the interior was beyond saving and much of what you see today was installed in the late 1960s, although the pulpit, organ and bell all date from the early 18th century. From St Kazimierz's walk down away from the square, cross Kościelna and you come to the Church of the Visitation of the Virgin Mary. *On the eastern side of the New Town Rynek.*

Church of the Visitation of the Virgin Mary

This is one of the very oldest churches in Warsaw, built in 1411, before the city

Church of the Holy Ghost on ul. Freta

The Church of the Visitation of the Virgin Mary

even became the capital of Mazovia. Legend has it that the construction of the church was paid for by a rich miller who'd been told by an angel in a dream to build a shrine on a snow-covered hill by the Vistula River in order to be blessed with his first son. There may be some truth in this legend; the church stands high on an outcrop of the Vistula scarp and has a large millstone fixed to the tower. Reconstructed from 1947 to 1966 in its original form, it's now the only authentic example of Mazovian Gothic architecture in the city and well worth a visit.
ul. Przyrynek 6.

Sapieha Palace

Back up Kościelna, turn right into ul. Zakroczymska and you'll see the

Sapieha Palace. Built between 1731 and 1746 at the order of the Chancellor of Great Lithuania, Jan Fryderyk Sapieha, the palace was designed by J Z Deybel, and is a rather nice example of late Baroque architecture. The two wings have kept their rococo styling and rich decoration of sculptures, but the courtyard has lost its gate. An extension was added as part of the remodelling in 1818–20, aimed at converting the palace into barracks for the 4th Infantry Regiment. After being burnt to the ground in 1944, it was reconstructed between 1950 and 1955 and became a school. Some of the original male statues were replaced by busts of women made by students of the Warsaw Academy of Fine Arts and modelled on the daughters of Maria Zachwatowiczowa, the woman responsible for the reconstruction work.

From the Sapieha Palace, walk straight down ul. Zakroczymska to the **Polish Security Printing Works** at ul. R Sanguszki 1. This is where all Polish banknotes are printed, as well as passports, identity cards and driving licences. From here you can look to your left towards the Polonia Football Ground on ul. Konwiktorska. A better alternative is to cross ul. R Sanguszki and have a stroll around **Romuald Traugutt Park**. This park includes the Citadel (*see pp54–5*) and is named after the leader of the January Uprising who was executed at Fort Legionów in 1864 along with other members of the

Temporary National Government. While here, have a look at the statue titled *Motherhood*. It's by Wacław Szymanowski, the same sculptor responsible for the Chopin Memorial in Royal Łazienki Park.

Sapieha Palace: ul. Zakroczymska 6. Not open to the public.

The Baroque façade of the Sapieha Palace

Walk: New Town

After being surrounded by half of Warsaw while walking around the Old Town (Stare Miasto), a stroll through the New Town (Nowe Miasto) is a refreshing change and one of the most picturesque trails on offer in the city. As you leave the Old Town, walk directly on to ul. Freta and follow it to reach the New Town Market Square (Rynek Nowego Miasta). Keep going to its end and take a right-hand turn down ul. Kościelna. Return to the square via St Benno's Church. Allow 90 minutes.

1 Ulica Freta

Freta is a charming street whose name is reputed to derive from the German *Freiheit* (freedom). To your right is the whitewashed **St Jacek's Church**, a Baroque structure, possibly designed by Giovanni Battista of Trevano, and rebuilt in the aftermath of World War II. The cobbled street is lined with one-room

bars and shops selling antiques (you cannot export antiques without a permit, *see pp144–5*), and is also home to a couple of Warsaw's more quirky museums.
Follow ul. Freta to No 5 – the Museum of Asia and Pacific.

2 Museum of Asia and Pacific

This is an extraordinary museum. Displays include mildly terrifying face masks from Oceania, jewellery from Uzbekistan, rugs from Afghanistan and a medley of other oddities you simply wouldn't dream of finding in a house on a quiet New Town street.
ul. Freta 5. Open: Wed & Fri–Sun 1–7pm, Tue & Thur 11am–5pm. Closed: Mon. Admission charge (except Thur). Keep on ul. Freta to No 16 – the Marie Curie Museum.

3 Marie Curie Museum

Housed in the building in which the Nobel Prize winner was born (*ul. Freta 16*), this four-room museum charts Maria Skłodowska-Curie's life as the

Map:

Church of the Visitation of the Virgin Mary
KOŚCIELNA
ZAKROCZYMSKA
Franciscan Monastery
Sapieha Palace
KOŚCIELNA
PRZYRYNEK
St Benno's Church
Church of St Francis Seraph
St Kazimierz's Church
RYNEK NOWEGO MIASTA
Podzamcze Park
FRETA
STARA
N
KOZLA
NEW TOWN (NOWE MIASTO)
Marie Curie Museum
Dominican Monastery
CASIA
ŚWIĘTOJERSKA
FRETA
Museum of Asia and Pacific
St Jacek's Church
MOSTOWA
★ Start of Walk
POI
Church of the Holy Ghost
Barbakan
NOWOMIEJSKA
0   100 metres
0   100 yards
PODWALE
DLUGA

scientist who discovered polonium and radium. It includes a diorama of her living room, awards for scientific work, personal letters and even her overcoat and handbag. Lab equipment and a range of international stamps commemorating her work are also displayed.

ul. Freta 16. Open: Tue 8.30am–4pm, Wed–Fri 9.30am–4pm, Sat 10am–4pm, Sun 10am–3pm. Closed: Mon. Admission charge.

Continue down ul. Freta and past the New Town Rynek to ul. Zakroczymska 1 – the Church of St Francis Seraph.

4 Church of St Francis Seraph

This is another Warsaw church with a history that manages to outdo the extravagant Baroque details. The remains of St Vitalis are kept in a glass coffin in a chapel to the left, with the adorning religious relics being gifts of Pope Benedict XIV in 1754. Built in 1679–1733, the church hosted the first Mass held in Warsaw following liberation from the Nazis.

From here, walk back in the direction you came, before taking a left turn on ul. Kościelna just before reaching the Rynek. Take a right turn where the street ends to reach ul. Piesza and the site of St Benno's Church.

5 St Benno's Church

St Benno's was founded in the 17th century to cater for the German-speaking community, also doubling as an orphanage during the 18th century.

Although King Zygmunt III was a devotee of St Benno, the local German population didn't have it easy; one story claims that the pastor, St Clemens Maria Hofbauer, was so strapped for cash he had to resort to begging in local bars for funds. Allegedly, one xenophobic local was so incensed by this that he spat in Hofbauer's beer, to which the latter replied, 'That was for me, now what are you going to give my boys?' His assailant was so overwhelmed with the response he raised 100 silver coins from those seated at the bar. The fact that St Benno's was a German church did little to save it during World War II, and it suffered the same fate as the rest of the area: razed to the ground in 1944.

Ulica Freta looking towards the Church of St Francis Seraph

The Gate of Execution of the Warsaw Citadel

The Citadel

On 29 November 1830 the people of Poland rose in rebellion against their Russian masters in what was to become known as the November Uprising. In spite of sporadic successes, Poland's military efforts proved disjointed and their leadership fractious; by October 1831 the dream of independence was crushed and the last Polish soldiers surrendered their arms. Stunned by this outbreak of insubordination, the Russian Tsar, Nicholas I, issued a firm response. On his orders a citadel was constructed to the north of the New Town. It was to serve a dual purpose: firstly to imprison those seen as a threat to the status quo; secondly to serve as a base for the Russian garrison. Over the next few decades it would become a symbol of Russian hegemony and Polish martyrdom.

Construction on the Citadel began immediately after the pacification of the November Uprising, its cornerstone laid by Field Marshal Ivan Paskevich, the man credited with suppressing the revolt. Designed by Major General Ivan Dehn, who took inspiration from a similar fortress in Antwerp, a pentagon-shaped red-brick stronghold was built enclosing a site of 36ha (89 acres). The people of Warsaw were furious; not only did the city have to foot the enormous bill, but more than 15,000 Varsovians were forcibly ejected from their homes to make way for the project. By 1834 the first Russian troops moved into their new premises, but public discontent continued to simmer. It reached boiling point in 1863 when a spontaneous protest against national conscription was brutally put down by Russian troops. Poland once more rose in revolt, this time in the January Uprising. The Citadel proved the trump card in the Russian efforts to subdue Warsaw; its 555 artillery positions covered vast swathes of the city, while the sheer size of the fortress allowed the garrison to swell to 16,000 soldiers. Captured insurgents filled the cells of the 'Tenth Pavilion', their numbers including Romuald Traugutt, the leader of the ill-fated revolt. His execution in 1864, carried out at what is now known as the Gate of Execution, was to prove a black day for patriots, more than 30,000 of whom turned up to witness his death.

During its 94 years serving as a prison, the Citadel saw approximately 40,000 people pass through its cells. Many of these went on to become household names: 'Red' Rosa Luxemburg, future Polish leader Józef Piłsudski, and Feliks Dzierżyński, who would later found the hated Soviet secret police, the KGB. The prison was closed in 1925, after which the Citadel became a military training ground, weapons depot and finally a museum in the 1960s. Much of it survived World War II, as well as earlier attempts to blow it up during World War I, and today its cells and narrow corridors are open to the public, filled with documents, paintings, letters and mugshots of famous prisoners. A cemetery has been added on the Citadel grounds to commemorate prisoners who lost their lives here, and there is a small collection of military hardware used by the Red Army during World War II.
ul. Skazańcow 25. Open: 9am–4pm. Closed Mon & Tue. Free admission.

Abandoned Russian cannon in the Citadel

Plac Krasińskich

Walk up the slight slope of ul. Długa from the New Town and you'll enter Krasińskich Square from its eastern corner. On your left is the **Field-Cathedral of the Polish Army**, on your right is the Monument to the Warsaw Uprising and, behind the monument, the Supreme Court building. Opposite the court is Krasińskich Palace.

Church of Our Lady Queen of Poland

This church is best known as the Field-Cathedral of the Polish Army, a confusing name given the large bronze propeller mounted next to the front. Poland doesn't officially have an army: it has 'Land Forces' that are part of the 'Armed Forces'. The church was built at the order of King Władysław IV in 1642 and was originally home to Piarist monks. Destroyed during the years of the deluge (1655–60), it was rebuilt in the Baroque style you see today. It has been the Field-Cathedral of the Polish Armed Forces since 1991, and many plaques on its walls commemorate Polish servicemen and women.

Krasińskich Palace

This is one of the largest and most beautiful palaces in the city. It was built between 1677 and 1695 for Jan Krasiński, the Voivode of Płock, and designed by Tylman of Gameren. After being purchased by the state in 1764, it served as the seat of the Treasury

The Church of Our Lady Queen of Poland

The Warsaw Uprising monument on Krasińskich Square; in the background the Supreme Court

Commission before suffering extensive fire damage in 1783 and becoming the residence of the Prussian authorities during the partition of Poland. When Poland regained its independence in 1918, the Supreme Court was based in the palace. Burnt and partially demolished by the Nazis in 1944, the palace has since been restored to its original form and is home to the Special Collections of the National Library. Architect and sculptor Andreas Schluter was responsible for the pediment reliefs and sculptures that make up the exterior decoration of the palace. Schluter also designed the Arsenal (*see p70*). Behind the palace is a park that has been open to the public since 1768.

pl. Krasińskich 5.
Palace not open to the public.

Monument to the Warsaw Uprising

For more than four decades the communist government refused to allow any monument to the Warsaw Uprising. When permission was finally given in the late 1980s, no funds were made available so the monument was paid for by donations from the public. It is in pl. Krasińskich because this is where the first shot of the Uprising was fired on 1 August 1944. Forty-five years later, to the day, the monument was unveiled. It shows two groups of insurgents: one defending a barricade and the other entering the sewers that they used for safe passage to the main Free Polish forces in the city centre.

Supreme Court building

Officially called 'The Complex of Justice at Krasińskich Square in Warsaw accommodating the Supreme Court at Krasińskich Square in Warsaw', this award-winning building caused controversy when it was built in the late 1990s. Some objected to the US$56 million it cost to build, others to the structure taking land from Krasińskich Park (*see p99*). Nowadays, it is widely regarded as one of Warsaw's finest modern buildings.

Not open to the public.

Plac Teatralny and Plac Bankowy

Plac Teatralny (Theatre Square) has for many years been the cultural heart of Warsaw. Located equidistant from the Old Town and the ghetto, it is far too often overlooked by visitors who are hurrying to see as many of the sights as possible in the shortest time. Warsaw simply does not suit that kind of visitor; you have to take your time to get the best from this city. Nowadays, the central business district has moved to the south, but Plac Bankowy still has some rather impressive architecture left over from its glory days.

Plac Teatralny

Many Varsovian buildings have served different functions over the years, and Plac Teatralny is no exception. It was initially an area for commerce, first earning significance during the late 17th century. At that time Warsaw was being rebuilt after the Swedish and Transylvanian armies had ravaged the city on three occasions in four years. The queen of the time, Queen Maria Sobieska, decided that the city needed a large-scale covered shopping area, a forerunner to modern-day shopping malls. The idea proved popular with Varsovians and in honour of the queen the centre was named Marywil (the Polish pronunciation of 'Marieville').

Bank of Poland building

The building at Bielińska 10/12, just a few steps north of pl. Teatralny, is one of the few remaining bombed-out buildings in the city. Constructed in 1907 as the Warsaw branch of the State Bank of the Russian Empire, it lasted only eight years in that role before all Russians were evacuated from Warsaw in 1915. The building passed to the Polish State Treasury and became the headquarters of the Bank of Poland when that was established in 1924. During the 1944 Uprising it was used as a base for the Home Army and therefore heavily bombed by the Nazis. Since then, a section of the building has been slightly renovated and given a temporary roof (quite a long time ago now) and the ground floor below has been partially renovated. The plan was for the renovated building to become home to the Warsaw Uprising Museum, but instead that is on ul. Przyokopowa (*see pp14–15*). So, despite being a hugely valuable piece of real estate, the building may remain a reminder of the Warsaw of 1945 for some time to come. *Bielińska 10/12.*

Jabłonowski Palace

In the early part of the 19th century, the city fathers decided the 400-year-old city hall was too old and decrepit. They purchased the Jabłonowski Palace on what is now pl. Teatralny and abandoned the old wooden building in the Rynek. Construction of the Jabłonowski Palace had taken some 12 years (1773–85), but the Jabłonowski family only had 32 years to enjoy their palace before it became the city hall. The palace was remodelled between 1864 and 1869 but was still in use as the city hall in 1939 when the mayor of Warsaw, Stefan Starzyński, commanded the defence of Warsaw and refused all offers to help him escape from the city and the certain death that awaited him when the Nazis captured him. Starzyński's bravery was one of the reasons he was voted Varsovian of the Century in 2003. The palace scarcely fared any better than Starzyński: heavily bombed in 1939, it suffered further damage in 1944 and was so far beyond repair that its remains were pulled down in 1952. Fortunately,

The ruins of the Bank of Poland building

capitalism has been fairly kind to the palace; it was rebuilt between 1995 and 1997. The façade and the tower are faithful reproductions of the originals, but the offices behind them are very modern and entirely suited to the palace's new role as a banking centre. *ul. Senatorska 14/16.*

Teatr Narodowy (National Theatre)

The theatre that gives pl. Teatralny its name is the huge Teatr Narodowy. Construction of the theatre started in 1825, to a classical design by Italian architect Antonio Corazzi, and took eight years to complete. The first performance was Gioachino Antonio Rossini's *The Barber of Seville*, which took place on 24 February 1833. The arts played an important role in sustaining the Polish nation during the long years of partition and the National Theatre was at the heart of that. Although subject to censorship from the Russian government throughout the 19th century, the theatre was where many of the most important Polish

The imposing rear of the National Theatre

FINISHING THE THEATRE

The National Theatre now features one element of the original design that was missing for nearly 200 years: Antonio Corazzi's original plans featured a sculpture of Apollo driving a chariot drawn by four horses. However, such a crowning glory was promptly vetoed by the Russian Field Marshal who ruled Warsaw; it was not in the interests of Russia for Poland to have a grand National Theatre. After the fall of communism the idea resurfaced of putting a statue where one had always been intended. The rector of the Warsaw Academy of Fine Arts, Adam Myjak, and the dean of the sculpture department, Antoni Janusz Pastwa, created a sculpture that was unveiled by President Aleksander Kwaśniewski on 3 May, Constitution Day, 2002.

works of the time were premiered. Good examples of such works include Stanisław Moniuszko's two best-known operas *Halka* and *The Haunted Manor*, first staged in 1858 and 1865 respectively.

The theatre was all but ruined during the 1939 bombing and was used as an execution ground during the 1944 Uprising. A small plaque on the right-hand side of the main entrance commemorates the deaths of the civilians killed there and the suffering of all victims of the Nazis. The damage was so extensive that although reconstruction work started in 1945, it was not until 19 November 1965 that the first post-war performance was held. The current form of the theatre was designed by Bohdan Pniewski and is a slightly expanded version of the original. The rear of the theatre was not reconstructed in as grand a form as before and now has a distinctly utilitarian feel to it. There are two reasonable restaurants, an interesting little café and one of Warsaw's most expensive clubs, but it also has a most unfortunate view of what has frequently been described as a monstrous carbuncle, the Metropolitan Building by Lord Foster (*see pp136–7*).

Colonnades flank both sides of the main entrance of the National Theatre

Plac Teatralny and Plac Bankowy

Plac Bankowy

Calling Plac Bankowy a square is more than slightly inaccurate: this is very much a rectangle and a rather squashed one at that. Sadly, the most impressive building, the Great Synagogue, was blown up by the Nazis in 1943 as a birthday present to Adolf Hitler. Apparently, it symbolised the eternal victory of the Aryan people over the Jews. The site is now covered by an uninspired glass-and-steel office block, known locally as the Blue Tower. Construction of the Blue Tower took nearly 30 years due to the project suffering an assortment of mysterious calamities. Varsovian myth has a tale about the site being cursed by a rabbi killed during the Ghetto Uprising and the building was only finished when another rabbi removed the curse in the late 1980s. For some fact to go with this fiction, pop into the **Jewish Historical Institute** in what was once the library of the Great Synagogue (*ul. Tłomackie 3/5, directly behind the Blue Tower*); the institute has some excellent displays and an interesting bookshop.

On the other side of ul. Marszałkowska, directly opposite the Blue Tower, is a building that appears to be suffering from a split-personality crisis: it's actually two palaces and a bank.

Bank of Poland and Stock Exchange building

Constructed in 1825–8 to plans by Antonio Corazzi, this is arguably the finest classically styled building in the city. The design is based around an operations room that is covered by a brass dome and has a twin-level arcade running around it. Badly damaged during World War II, it was rebuilt and in 1957 became the home of the Museum of the History of the Polish Revolutionary Movement. That museum was closed shortly before martial law was imposed in 1981. After the fall of communism in 1990, a replacement was opened: the John Paul II art collection, more than 450 works by various world-famous talents.

The Blue Tower on pl. Bankowy

The Palace of Treasury Ministers and statue of Juliusz Słowacki

Palace of the Governmental Commission for Revenues and Treasury

A grandiose and complex title, but what else would you expect bureaucrats to name their office block? The building itself is also rather grand with its rows of tall columns, but its look isn't improved by the courtyard being used as a car park. Currently, this is where the mayor of Warsaw, Hanna Gronkiewicz-Waltz, has her offices. There were plans to move the mayor's office to Saski Palace (currently being reconstructed on pl. Piłsudskiego), but the city council has a habit of planning what doesn't happen and not planning what does happen.

Palace of Treasury Ministers

This was built at the same time as the Bank of Poland and Stock Exchange building but on a rather larger scale and with considerably more majesty, as would befit one of the government's most senior members. After being rebuilt with little care and attention, the palace was recently given a thorough renovation and is back to its best.

Tour: Bus No 180

Bus No 180 is an ideal choice for visitors: it runs close to many of the city's main attractions, from Powązki Cemetery to pl. Zamkowy and down the Royal Route all the way to Wilanów Palace (see pp130, 34–5, 82–93 and 134–5, respectively). The journey from Powązki to Wilanów takes between 50 and 70 minutes. Buy a 24-hour ticket (PLN7.20 and valid on all public transport); you can easily spend all day hopping on and off bus No 180.

1 Ulica Bednarska and Mariensztat

Get off at the pl. Zamkowy stop and head down ul. Bednarska to the small but perfectly formed Mariensztat district. Both once had less than salubrious reputations: ul. Bednarska was well known for its brothels and Mariensztat for bare-knuckle boxing. The area was flattened during World War II and today looks rather different from the old Mariensztat; it was the first part of Warsaw to be rebuilt and redesigned as a showpiece for socialism. It quickly became the most desirable address in Warsaw but today has faded much faster than the Old Town. In parts a little shabby, the wonderful thing is it's almost entirely free of tourists.

Back up ul. Bednarska, either walk 500m (550yds) down Krakowskie Przedmieście or take bus No 180 two stops from pl. Zamkowy and you're at the main campus of Warsaw University.

2 Warsaw University

There are too many interesting buildings on the campus to mention; your best bet is to have a wander around.

Return to bus route 180 and jump off next at the Foksal stop and stroll down to Rondo de Gaulle'a.

3 Rondo de Gaulle'a

To your left are a **statue of General Charles de Gaulle** and the former headquarters of the Polish United Workers' Party. After the fall of communism it was turned, ironically, into the home of the Warsaw **Stock Exchange**.

Walk into pl. Trzech Krzyży (see pp90–91); the bus stop is at the far end where the square joins al. Ujazdowskie.

4 Chopin Memorial and Royal Łazienki Park

Get off at the Łazienki Królewskie stop and go in through the gates of Royal Łazienki Park. The first thing you see is the world-famous Chopin

Memorial. The statue was made by Wacław Szymanowski in 1908 but was not placed in its current position until 1926. It was dynamited by the Nazis in May 1940, one of the first monuments in Warsaw to be destroyed. Local legend says that the next day in its place was a handwritten sign that read 'I don't know who destroyed me but I know why: so I don't play the funeral march for your leader.' A cast of the original statue survived the war, enabling an exact reproduction to be put up in the same place in 1958.

From here, go back to the bus stop and either take bus No 180 south all the way to Wilanów Palace (see pp134–5) or north back to the city centre. Alternatively, walk down the hill behind the statue and have a wander around the park or follow the route suggested on pp100–101.

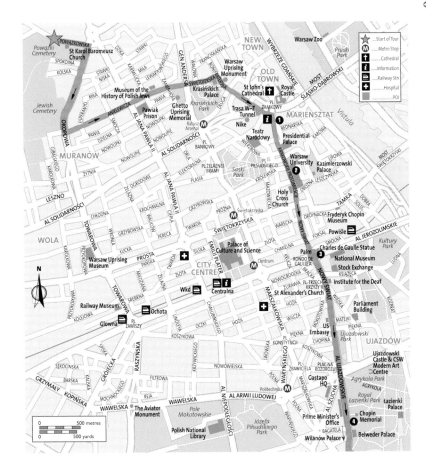

Oś Saska (The Saxon Axis)

Oś Saska is another feature of historical Warsaw often missed by visitors. King Augustus II came up with the idea of creating a line of palaces and parks running from the Vistula River to pl. Żelaznej Bramy. Inspiration for his plan was the design of the Versailles complex outside Paris, and the project was to cover a significant section of Warsaw. Despite the efforts of Augustus II and his son, Augustus III, the project was never completed.

This was mainly due to the high cost, although it is possible that both kings had other things on their minds: Augustus II had a dozen children with a variety of women; his son matched that number but all were born within his one marriage. The centrepieces of the Saxon Axis were completed: a palace and a large park that was open to the public. Both the park and the palace were named after the Saxon origins of the kings: Saski Park and Saski Palace – *Saski* is the Polish word for 'Saxon'.

Saski Palace

The first step in the plan for the Saxon Axis was to purchase the Morsztynów family palace. What was a fairly modest structure (as palaces go) was significantly expanded; the body and two wings of the new palace covered the entire square. Unfortunately, the palace had a less than successful history; in 1842 its front gardens and gates were flattened on the orders of the then Russian governor, Prince Constantin, to make space for his favourite hobby: military parades. In 1894 the central section of the palace was pulled down so that the Alexander Nevsky Russian Orthodox Cathedral could be constructed in its place. After World War I the palace became the headquarters of the Polish army, and in December 1932 it was where the Enigma codes of the German armed forces were first broken. World War II brought the almost total destruction of the palace. The only part left standing was a section with three of the lower arches of the colonnade that connected the two symmetrical wings of the palace. By chance, the middle of those three arches had since 1925 been the site of the **Tomb of the Unknown Soldier**. Despite surviving the war, the tomb only partially survived the peace: the tablets commemorating the Polish–Bolshevik War of 1920 were removed and only reinstalled in 1990 after the fall of communism.

Work to reconstruct the palace started in 2006 with an initial completion date of 2009. However, problems with excavation work uncovering significant archaeological remains, plus budgetary concerns, led to work being halted and the site returned to its previous state. Work is scheduled to start again in 2013.

Plac Piłsudskiego

This square is now back to the second of its four names. Originally called pl. Saski when it was created in the 19th century, its name was changed in the early 20th century to honour Marshal Józef Piłsudski, first leader of newly independent Poland. Between

1939 and 1945 the name was Adolf Hitler Platz, and then pl. Zwycięstwa (Victory Square) during the communist era, before reverting to pl. Piłsudskiego. Recent times have not been architecturally kind to the square: after losing the Saski Palace it was blighted in 1976 with the concrete block that is the **Victoria Hotel** (although the hotel does have a good piano bar) and then cursed with the monstrous **Metropolitan Building** in 2003. Hopefully the reconstruction of the Saski Palace and the neighbouring Brühl Palace (originally built in 1642) will be completed in the not too distant future.

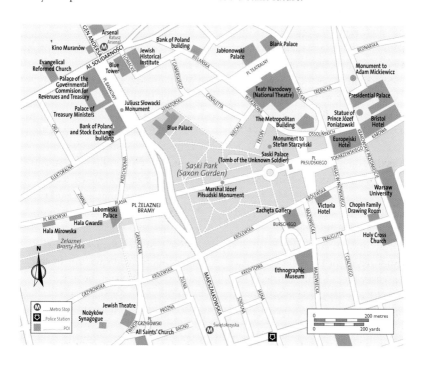

The lake and water tower in Saski Park

Saski Park

This park was first opened to the public in 1727 and so is one of the oldest public parks in the world. Originally laid out in the French-inspired Baroque style popular in the early 1700s, it was remodelled during the mid-18th century in the English landscape garden style. Despite the attention of the Nazis from 1939 to 1944, several classic features of this remodelling remain today or have been rebuilt: the temple on a small hill (in reality a well-disguised water tower), the small lake and the pseudo-meadow. The original Baroque design has not completely disappeared; the Saxon Axis through the park is still covered with

ENRICO 'HENRYK' MARCONI

The Saxon Axis features three works by Enrico Marconi. Better known in Poland as 'Henryk' Marconi, he was one of the more talented and active architects in 19th-century Warsaw. In 1859 pl. Piłsudskiego was graced by his elegantly designed Europejski Hotel (*see pp85–6*). In Saski Park, just behind the Tomb of the Unknown Soldier, is a delightful fountain designed in the empire style and recently completely renovated. The park is also home to his water tower disguised as a Greek temple. Unfortunately, few of his buildings were restored after World War II, but All Saints' Church on pl. Grzybowski (*see p71*) was rebuilt and shows the genius of the man. His son, Leandro Marconi, also became an architect and created a number of beautiful Warsaw buildings.

symmetrically designed flowerbeds. Also worth seeing are Marconi's fountain, a sundial that has counted every minute since 1863 (every minute of sunlight anyway), and the statue of of Stefan Starzyński, former mayor of Warsaw. Slightly off the axis is the **Blue Palace** on the corner of the park by pl. Bankowy. Despite its name, the current form of the palace is somewhat drab; regrettably, the original elegant, blue, rococo-style structure is now just a memory. However, given that the palace is now the home of the municipal transport authority, perhaps drab is fitting.

Plac Żelaznej Bramy (Iron Gate Square)

Back on the axis and across ul. Marszałkowska is an interesting relic of Varsovian history. As part of Augustus II's plan, the wooden houses that stood here were demolished and replaced with a large gateway with an iron gate. The plan called for **Lubomirski Palace** also to be demolished because it faced 30 degrees away from the axis; fortunately, funds ran out before the palace was pulled down. After World War II the iron gate was not rebuilt but the palace was rotated so that it now faces straight back down the axis.

The fountain in Saski Park designed by Enrico 'Henryk' Marconi

Walk: Around the Saxon Axis

The area east of the Saxon Axis has some interesting sights but is ignored by virtually all visitors. Start at the Arsenal by Ratusz Metro Station and walk along al. Solidarności past two rather unusual churches to al. Jana Pawła II. A few steps down al. Jana Pawła II brings you to Hala Mirowska. Walk through the park alongside those buildings and down ul. Graniczna to pl. Grzybowski.

Allow 2 hours.

1 Arsenal

Warsaw's Arsenal was built in the 16th century and reconstructed in 1638–43. Twice rebuilt in the 1700s, it was damaged in the 1794 Uprising and converted into a prison. A stronghold of the Home Army during the Warsaw Uprising, it was entirely destroyed in 1944. What you see today was built in 1948–50 and is a re-creation of the mid-17th-century building.
Cross ul. Andersa via Ratusz Metro station and follow the signs for Muranów.

2 Kino Muranów

Opened in 1951, this cinema takes its name from the post-war Muranów development (*see p76*). It has built a reputation as the venue of choice for film fans. Outside is a fountain dating from 1866, now dedicated to the Wigry battalion of the Home Army.
Walk to the corner of ul. Andersa and turn right on to al. Solidarności. The Evangelical Reformed Church is at No 74.

3 Evangelical Reformed Church

Arguably the most beautiful church in Warsaw, this dates back to 1776 and originally held services in Polish, German and French. The acoustics inside are superb and the church hosts regular choral concerts.
Walk straight down al. Solidarności from the Evangelical Reformed Church to the Church of the Nativity at No 80.

4 Church of the Nativity

This church was constructed in the 17th century for the adjoining Carmelite monastery. Rebuilt after World War II, it is most remarkable because the entire church was moved backwards by 21m (69ft) overnight (30 November to 1 December) in 1962 as part of work to widen al. Solidarności.
Turn left down al. Jana Pawła II and walk towards the central railway station.

5 Hala Mirowska and Hala Gwardii

These two identical halls were built between 1899 and 1901 at the order of

the mayor of Warsaw, Nikolai Bibikov. Although both suffered serious fire damage during World War II, their massive brick walls survived and the halls were rebuilt. After a short stint as Warsaw's bus depot in the late 1940s, they became state-run markets. Outside is a flower market, a good meat market and excellent fruit and vegetable stalls.
Walk along the halls to pl. Żelaznej Bramy, then right into ul. Graniczna and down to pl. Grzybowski.

6 Plac Grzybowski

This small square is home to **All Saints' Church**, the **Jewish Theatre** and, behind the theatre, the **Nożyków Synagogue** (*see pp146–7 and p74, respectively*). All Saints', the work of Enrico Marconi, dates from 1861. It was one of three Catholic churches in the ghetto; the others were the Church of the Nativity (*see opposite*) and St Augustine's at ul. Nowolipki 18 (*see p76 & p78*). Nożyków Synagogue is the work of Enrico's son, Leandro.

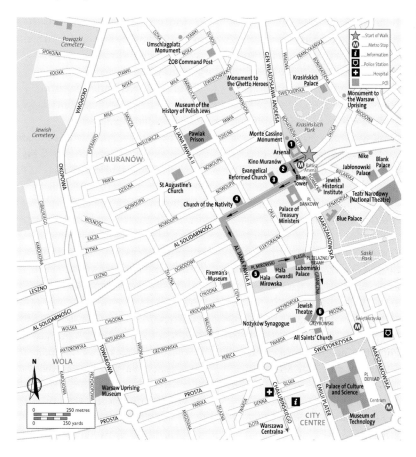

The Ghetto Uprising

In 1943 (a year before the Warsaw Uprising) the last Jews living in the Warsaw ghetto rose up to take on the might of the Nazi army. But while the Warsaw Uprising was genuinely aimed at defeating the Nazis, none of the Ghetto Uprising insurgents had any illusions about their ability to win a military victory.

The Jewish ghetto in Warsaw was formed in 1940, when nearly 400,000 Jews were herded into one part of the city. The area was soon enclosed by a tall brick wall, which was topped with barbed wire and closely guarded.

Conditions were cramped and disease was rampant among the malnourished inhabitants.

The ghetto was divided into a smaller and larger area separated by ul. Chłodna along which other residents of Warsaw could move freely. At first, there were gates between the two parts of the ghetto, but later a bridge was built between the two sides, reducing any contact between Jews and other Varsovians.

In 1942 Jews began to be deported from the ghetto in huge numbers. The Jewish authorities decided not to fight

The bridge joining the two parts of the ghetto

against this, despite being urged to by Jewish youth groups, because the authorities believed the camps were labour camps rather than anything more sinister. However, by the time the Nazis started the second wave of deportations in 1943, reports of what was actually happening at the camps had filtered back to the ghetto. The Jews decided that they had no choice but to fight back. As deportation meant certain death, fighting back, even with its microscopic chance of success, would constitute an honourable way to die.

Following gun battles in January 1943, during which Jews resisted deportation and halted the Nazis' plans, even if only briefly, the inhabitants of the ghetto prepared to fight over a prolonged period of time. They dug bunkers connected to the sewage system, collected arms and divided themselves into military districts, each with its own organisational system. Because the ghetto was so isolated from the rest of Warsaw, limited support got through from the outside, although Polish resistance units from the Home Army (Armia Krajowa, the AK) managed to fight alongside the Jews on several occasions and smuggled limited numbers of weapons to them.

Between 19 April and 16 May 1943, the Jews made a concerted effort to rise up against the Nazis.

April saw most of the actual fighting, but the ghetto inhabitants were poorly armed and in bad physical shape. Once the Nazis began destroying buildings by setting fire to block after block, the resistance was driven underground, into its bunkers. The Nazis used incendiary grenades and poisonous gas to drive people out of their hideouts. At the beginning of May the bunker that held the headquarters of the Jewish Fighting Organisation (Żydowska Organizacja Bojowa, ŻOB) was discovered. Most ŻOB members, including leader Mordechai Anielewicz, committed suicide.

Following the uprising, the 50,000 people who remained (after around 13,000 had been killed in the fighting, burnt alive or gassed in the bunkers) were sent to death camps.

A few escaped this fate and continued sporadic attacks against the Nazis, surviving in the sewers and joining the Warsaw Uprising the following year. The area that once held the ghetto was used by the Nazis to establish the Warsaw Concentration Camp. When the Warsaw Uprising began, this camp was seized by the Home Army (on 5 August 1944) and 360 prisoners, mainly Jews, were freed. Virtually all of them immediately joined the Home Army and the fight against the Nazis.

The Former Ghetto

In 1939 the Jewish community in Warsaw numbered approximately 440,000. By 1945 that number was only 20. More than a third of the city's population had gone, 90 per cent of them were dead and few of the survivors would ever return to Warsaw. What was once the Jewish quarter had been systematically razed to the ground. A thousand years of history was wiped out in five years.

Before 1939 Jews accounted for 10 per cent of the population of Poland and mainly lived in the larger cities. Jewish scientists were among the leading experts in both Poland and Europe. After World War I the first Polish parliament included a Jewish party with 35 members and Poland's first female member of parliament, Roza Pomerantz-Meltzer. Many of the prominent figures in the medical and business world were Jewish. The majority of Warsaw's Jews lived in the northeastern part of the city, centred around the Muranów district. The name Muranów comes from the Baroque Murano Palace that was built on ul. Inflancka in the mid-17th century by a wealthy royal architect, Joseph Bellotti. Bellotti named his palace after the island in Venice that his family came from. Venice was also the origin of this area's less attractive name: the ghetto (the first Jewish ghetto was created in Venice in 1516).

Although the vast majority of the ghetto was demolished street by street and house by house, a few traces remain. Those wishing to snatch a glimpse of part of the ghetto wall can do so at ul. Sienna 55. Note that it's found in a residential courtyard, so you may have to ring a few door bells to gain entry if the main gate is locked.

Other surviving elements of the ghetto include the **Nożyków Synagogue** (*ul. Twarda 6*). Pre-war Warsaw had dozens of synagogues; post-war Warsaw has just one and it only survived because Nazi officers demonstrated their famed sense of humour by using the building for stabling their horses. The synagogue is now in daily use but is open to visitors every afternoon except Saturday. Next to the synagogue, at pl. Grzybowski 12/16, is the **Jewish Theatre**, the only Yiddish-language theatre in Europe (*see pp146–7*).

Plac Grzybowski is also where one of Warsaw's most authentic post-war streets, or at least a fragment of it, can be found: ul. Próżna. Pre-1939 the area was home to both tradesmen and shopkeepers, and doctors and lawyers. The building at No 7 housed Lipszyc's Department Store. Zalman Nożyk (who founded the Nożyków Synagogue, hence it taking his name) owned the hardware store at No 9. The Warsaw Bolt and Wire Factory had its home at No 14, and even today the street keeps its traditional trade in nails and screws. Unfortunately, the buildings are more or less in the same condition as they were in 1945. The only obvious additions are the large wooden boards attached at the level of the ground-floor ceilings: those are there to catch bits of the building as they fall off. Plans have been put forward to restore the buildings and to redevelop the area (the prime real estate at the corner of ul. Marszałkowska and ul. Świętokrzyska is currently occupied by shacks selling kebabs and sex toys), but until the issue of who exactly owns it has been cleared up, nothing can happen. Poland's record on providing restitution to people who lost their property during and after World War II should be a national disgrace.

To the north of pl. Grzybowski, much of the street plan has changed since 1944. So little was left standing that the planners had a virtually blank sheet to work with. To get an idea of

Ulica Próżna seen from pl. Grzybowski

St Augustine's Church seen from the Evangelical Reformed Church in 1945

the scale of the devastation, head north along al. Jana Pawła II to ul. Nowolipki. Turn right into ul. Nowolipki and you'll see that the ground-floor level of the buildings on either side is more than 1m (3ft) higher than the surface of the road. Those hills are not natural formations. The architect responsible for designing the post-war district, Bohdan Lachert, used the rubble of the ghetto to make the Muranów development. What appear to be the hills that form elevated terraces are actually the remnants of the ground floors of pre-war buildings that were covered with soil. The buildings that sit atop the piles of rubble are themselves constructed from breeze blocks made

from crushed rubble and concrete. Another place where these artificial terraces can be seen is al. Solidarności between pl. Bankowy and al. Jana Pawła II: the buildings on the northern side of the road have ground floors 2m (6½ft) above those on the southern side. Lachert's supporters claim that rubble was used so extensively in order to reflect the idea of rebirth of the city, Warsaw returning to life like a phoenix from the ashes. However, his critics say that it was used because there was no money to cart the stuff away and very little money for any other building materials either. Residents are usually too busy putting plaster over the cracks in their walls to make any comment.

An artificial terrace in Muranów built from the ruins of the ghetto

The notorious Pawiak Prison

Although the devastation Muranów suffered was greater than that of central Hiroshima, ul. Nowolipki is also where you can find one of the very few structures that predates World War II: **St Augustine's Church** (*ul. Nowolipki 18*). Originally built in the 19th century for Jews who converted to Catholicism (often in an attempt to assimilate), it survived both the Ghetto Uprising and the destruction of the area that followed. Some historians claim it was left standing in order not to anger the Catholic population of Warsaw. Others think this motive unlikely, and conclude that it stayed only because it was a location from which a small team of snipers could ensure that nobody moved in the entire area. The latter explanation is rather more likely to be true.

It's also in the Muranów district that visitors can follow the Passion Road: a path of remembrance that twists its way through the streets of the former Jewish ghetto, its route marked by 16 granite blocks that tell the story of the Ghetto Uprising in Polish, Hebrew and Yiddish. Many of these blocks recall the heroic figures that arose during the years of suffering. These include **Doctor Janusz Korczak**, a well-known educator and children's author who

THE PIANIST

The Pianist is Władysław Szpilman's biographical account of life in the Warsaw ghetto. Originally banned in post-war Poland, the book shot to international fame after Roman Polański turned it into an Oscar-winning epic. A concert pianist for Polish radio, Szpilman's life was turned upside down when Warsaw fell to the Nazis and he was trapped inside Europe's biggest ghetto. The book offers stunning insight into ghetto life as well as his amazing battle for survival. Smuggled into the Aryan quarter after witnessing the deportation of his family, Szpilman's life was saved by a Nazi officer. A classic book and a must-read.

also dedicated his time to running an orphanage. Just before he and his young charges were transported to Treblinka, he was offered the chance to save his life but instead chose to remain with his orphans, accompanying them to their deaths in the gas chambers. Others immortalised in stone include **Emanuel Ringelblum**, an active social leader who strove to ease conditions in the ghetto. Executed by the Nazis in 1944, two years later ten metal boxes belonging to him were found in the rubble of Warsaw. They were filled with his personal diaries chronicling life in the ghetto; these tomes are now regarded as crucial historical documents. Finally, look for the memorial at ul. St Dubois 5 dedicated to **Szmul Zygielbojm**, a member of the Polish National Council who committed suicide in London in 1943 in protest against the perceived passivity with which the world was facing Nazi crimes. Addressed to Allied and Polish leaders, his suicide letter declared: 'I cannot continue to live and be silent while the remnants of Polish Jewry are being murdered. My comrades in the Warsaw ghetto fell with weapons in their hands in the last heroic battle. I was not permitted to fall like them, but I belong with them, in their mass grave.'

The Nożyków Synagogue, next to the Jewish Theatre on pl. Grzybowski

To begin the Passion Walk, start at **Pawiak** (*ul. Dzielna 24/26*), a prison constructed in the 1830s by the ruling Tsarist regime. It achieved notoriety during World War II when it served as a political prison holding members of the Polish intelligentsia and resistance movement. More than 100,000 prisoners passed through the gates, with over a third executed within the grounds. Although the bulk of the buildings were blown up during the Nazi retreat, the cramped cells have been reconstructed and a subterranean hall now contains a small but powerful museum. The gloomy exhibition includes mugshots of many of the victims, as well as personal effects such as improvised playing cards, chess sets,

GESTAPO HQ

Although unlikely to take more than 20 minutes, a visit to the former Gestapo HQ (*al. Szucha 25*) gives a sobering insight into Nazi terror. Originally built in 1930 to serve as a religious centre, the building was commandeered by the Nazis and for the next few years became the most dreaded address in Warsaw. Its murky basements functioned as an interrogation centre and have been faithfully preserved. On show is a stirring memorial as well as a few holding cells riddled with bullet holes, where prisoners would await their fate.

poetry and letters. The commemorative tree that stands outside is covered with prisoners' obituaries, placed in the immediate aftermath of liberation.

Across al. Jana Pawła II and penned in by ul. Karmelicka and ul. Zamenhofa (so named after Ludwik Zamenhof, the Jewish professor who dreamt up the Esperanto language) is a small park, its centrepiece being the **Monument to the Ghetto Heroes**. The bleak memorial was unveiled in 1948 and its reliefs depict a group of Jews being marched to their death on one side, and a team of resistance fighters on the other. Interestingly, the stone cladding used on the monument was originally imported from Sweden by the Nazis to make the victory arch that was to sit in the centre of Nazi Warsaw after the war. An identical replica stands in Israel's Yad Vashem. It's also in this park that the **Museum of the History of Polish Jews** is due to take root. Designed by a pair of Finnish architects, the museum was originally scheduled to open in

Monument to the Ghetto Heroes

2008, but the delays that plague virtually every project in Warsaw have taken their inevitable toll and the opening is currently planned for 2012. When completed, the multimedia museum aims to recount the 1,000-year history of Polish Jews, with eight separate sections to peruse. For a preview, visit the excellent website at *www.jewishmuseum.org.pl*

Across the crossroads between ul. Miła and ul. Zamenhofa is a monument to the former command post used by Jewish resistance leaders during the Ghetto Uprising. Keep your eyes open – it's well hidden among residential blocks, and is little more than a mound of earth with a staircase that leads to an engraved stone. It's here that the Jewish Fighting Organisation (Żydowska Organizacja Bojowa, ŻOB) had their

headquarters, and where their leader Mordechai Anielewicz commited suicide moments before capture.

Some 300,000 Jews from the ghetto were gassed in the Treblinka death camp. The spot where they were transported to their deaths, known as Umschlagplatz, is now marked by a sombre monument found on ul. Stawki. The work of architect Hanna Szmalenberg and sculptor Władysław Klamerus, the ***Umschlagplatz* Monument** was unveiled in 1988 with the aim of resembling a cattle wagon with its doors open. Walk inside to escape the traffic noise and view white marble walls engraved with thousands of Jewish names running from A to Z. The deportations, which would transport up to 7,000 people daily, finally ceased on 12 September 1942.

The impressive monument *Umschlagplatz* on ul. Stawki

Around the Royal Route

The royal route stretches from the Royal Castle on pl. Zamkowy to the royal residence at Wilanów. Krakowskie Przedmieście and Nowy Świat form the first part of the route and are two of present-day Warsaw's more beautiful streets. They give an idea of what the city looked like before suffering the attention of Nazi miscreants and the rebuilding by the Soviets.

Krakowskie Przedmieście

Krakowskie Przedmieście translates as 'Kraków Suburb' (it runs pretty much southwards and thus more or less in the general direction of Kraków). After construction of the Royal Castle started in the 16th century, the street became a very desirable area for the richer members of the aristocracy to have their palaces, or their town palaces anyway. The sacking of Warsaw by the Swedish army three times in the mid-17th century led to a large amount of building land becoming suddenly available (once the ruins of the old buildings had been pulled down), and so up went many of the elegant structures that you can see today. Krakowskie Przedmieście is also home to the main campus of Warsaw University, the Presidential Palace, two of Warsaw's finest hotels, and numerous palaces, churches, government buildings and houses. The ground floors of many of the houses are now occupied by upmarket shops and restaurants that often prove that price is no guarantee of quality.

Krakowskie Przedmieście seen from outside Warsaw University

St Anne's Church

Dating from 1454, this church has been burnt down three times (twice accidentally and once, in 1657, deliberately), bombed by the Nazis

Around the Royal Route

and very nearly destroyed by the communists. This makes it rather hard to understand the church's status as a 'lucky' church for weddings. Much of the present-day façade was constructed in 1788 by Chrystian Peter Aigner and is in the Baroque-Classicist style popular at that time. When the Trasa W-Z Tunnel (*see p34*) was being built, the church came close to collapsing because its foundations were compromised. The city authorities employed Professor Romuald Cebertowicz to use his electro-osmosis process to dry and solidify the soil under the church. They also employed a rather more traditional approach: 400 builders working night and day for two weeks to put steel-reinforced concrete beams under the church. Cebertowicz's electro-osmosis technique was also used to stop the Leaning Tower of Pisa from leaning too much. It's worth stopping at St Anne's just to climb up the bell tower: the view is one of the best in Warsaw.
ul. Krakowskie Przedmieście 68.

Monument to Adam Mickiewicz

A little way down Krakowskie Przedmieście from St Anne's, the Monument to Adam Mickiewicz (*see p84*) was constructed to commemorate the 100th anniversary of his birth and so was unveiled in 1898. Among the leaders of the committee responsible for the monument was Henryk Sienkiewicz, later to win the Nobel Prize for literature. As a symbol of Polish culture, the monument suffered

particularly close interest from the Nazis (bullet holes can still be seen in the plinth) and the statue was eventually carted off for scrap. Mickiewicz's head was found in a Hamburg scrapyard and formed the basis of the reconstructed statue unveiled in 1950.

Statue of Prince Józef Poniatowski

Prince Józef Poniatowski was one of Napoleon's generals, hence this statue portraying him as a classical hero, complete with Roman-style armour and tunic. Its unveiling was cancelled due to the 1830 November Uprising

ADAM MICKIEWICZ

Although he's not well known outside Poland, Adam Mickiewicz (1798–1855) is beloved by Poles and widely considered the greatest Polish writer of all time. Comparisons with Shakespeare would not be inappropriate. Perhaps one of the reasons for the high esteem in which he is held here was his devotion to Poland and his refusal to do as he was told by foreign powers. Exiled to central Russia at the age of twenty-six, he moved to Germany five years later and never saw Poland again. A good deal of rumour surrounds much of his life but all agree that he died in Turkey in 1855 while organising a military unit called the Hussars of Israel to fight for Polish independence.

and the statue was moved to Modlin Fortress before being taken to Belarus in 1840 by Russian general Ivan Paskevich, who put it in his garden. In 1922 it was returned to Warsaw but then totally destroyed in World War II. The current statue was a gift from the people of Copenhagen in 1965 and has stood outside the Presidential Palace ever since.

Presidential Palace

First built in 1643–5 as the residence of the Hetman (commander-in-chief of the Polish army) of the time, Stanisław Koniecpolski, the palace's current form is a result of the remodelling carried out in 1818–19 according to Chrystian Peter Aigner's neoclassical design. After that alteration it became the residence of the Viceroy of Congress Poland. Between 1939 and 1944 it was known as Deutsches Haus but did survive

Monument to Adam Mickiewicz

The Bristol Hotel, designed by Leandro Marconi

the Warsaw Uprising without significant damage. Following World War II it was the seat of the Polish Council of Ministers, and the Warsaw Pact was signed here in 1955. The Round Table Talks of 1989 (*see p13*) were also held here. Since July 1994 it has been the official residence of the Polish president.
ul. Krakowskie Przedmieście 46/48.

Bristol Hotel and Europejski Hotel
The two hotels that have long battled for the title 'Best Hotel in Warsaw' stand opposite each other on Krakowskie Przedmieście: the Bristol and the Europejski. The Europejski is the older of the two, built in 1855–9 (with finishing work done 1876–7); the Bristol was built in 1899–1901. Both hotels were designed by members of the Marconi family: the Europejski by Enrico 'Henryk' Marconi (*see p68*) and the Bristol by Enrico's son, Leandro 'Władysław' Marconi. Both hotels suffered very badly during World War II and after it. The Bristol was seriously damaged, much of its original Art Nouveau interior was replaced with low-quality socialist-realist rubbish, and the hotel shut down in 1981. After an extensive reconstruction programme, it reopened in 1993 and has been one of Warsaw's most luxurious hotels ever

The Krakowskie Przedmieście gates to Warsaw University

since. The Europejski's troubles are not yet over. Also seriously damaged during the war, it was rebuilt as a military academy before being opened as a hotel in 1962. After a 15-year battle against Polish authorities, the pre-war owners recovered the hotel in 2006. Renovation work began in 2008 and, after 60 million euros have been spent, the Europejski will reopen in 2011 (an unofficial goal is New Year's Eve 2010 to commemorate its original opening on 31 December 1856). The two hotels can then resume their rivalry after a 70-year break.
Bristol Hotel: ul. Krakowskie Przedmieście 42/44. Europejski Hotel: ul. Krakowskie Przedmieście 13.

Warsaw University

Warsaw University dates back to 1816. Originally, it had five departments, but all were closed in 1831 after the November Uprising. It reopened in 1857 but was again closed after the 1863 January Uprising. Between 1870 and 1915 it was the Imperial University of Warsaw and all classes were in Russian. After reverting to the Polish language, the university was closed during World War II. It was the scene of heavy fighting during the Warsaw Uprising and lost some 60 per cent of its buildings along with 80 per cent of its collections. The post-war communist government wasted little time introducing criteria aimed at ensuring that only politically correct professors and students entered Warsaw University. However, despite constant attention from the communist-era Ministerstwo Bezpieczeństwa Publicznego (Ministry of Public

Security, better known as the Secret Police) and the brutal suppression of student protests in March 1968 against the anti-Semitic policies of the government, the university was a major centre of the democratic movement. *ul. Krakowskie Przedmieście 26/28.*

Nicolas Copernicus Monument
Marking where ul. Krakowskie Przedmieście becomes Nowy Świat, this monument was erected in 1830 and is the work of Danish sculptor Berthel Thorvaldsen, also responsible for Prince Józef Poniatowski's statue. It shows Copernicus holding a spherical astrolabe that demonstrates his theory of heliocentrism. During World War II the Nazis covered the monument's Polish-language carvings with brass plaques in German. These were

NICOLAS COPERNICUS

Born in Toruń, Poland, in 1473, Nicolas Copernicus is often called the founder of the theory of Copernican heliocentrism, as put forward in his book *De Revolutionibus Orbium Coelestium*. Poles have a much better way of describing him: the man who stopped the sun and moved the earth. His theory flew in the face of conventional wisdom and, more importantly, what the Catholic Church decreed to be true. Copernicus avoided meeting the same fate as many of his supporters (being convicted of heresy and burnt at the stake) by having the good sense to hold the publication of his magnum opus until very shortly before his death. Apparently somebody did expect the Spanish Inquisition.

promptly removed by Maciej Dawidowski, a scoutmaster and member of the Home Army. The statue was removed by the Nazis to be melted down for scrap metal but was found in

Nicolas Copernicus: the man who stopped the sun and moved the earth

Around the Royal Route

Nysa in western Poland at the end of the war and returned to its place on Krakowskie Przedmieście. Thorvaldsen made two other statues from the same mould: one is in Chicago, the other in Montreal.

Nowy Świat

Nowy Świat means 'New World' and this street dates back to the mid-17th century. Then it was the main street out of town, and how the aristocracy reached their palaces and villas. But Warsaw at that time was growing rapidly and by the end of the same century the street had been paved and was lined by wooden houses of varying size and grandeur.

These wooden houses were soon replaced by more substantial structures. Just 100 years after it got its name, Nowy Świat already had seven palaces and more than two dozen town houses, all built along neoclassical lines and mostly three storeys high. Although the years of partition were not kind to Poland in general, Nowy Świat grew markedly in importance. It became the principal business street in Warsaw and it was one of the first streets in the city to have gas streetlights, installed in 1856. Part of the cost of this extravagance was met by the shopkeepers of the street. One of those shops still survives today, a delightful little pharmacy near the corner of Nowy Świat and ul. Smolna.

By 1918 virtually all of the original neoclassical houses had been replaced by larger, mainly Art Nouveau-style buildings, some of which were six storeys high.

World War II left Nowy Świat in very bad shape; not a single building escaped unscathed and most were utterly ruined. The city authorities decided to rebuild the street in its early 19th-century form, largely due to the

Shops and restaurants on Nowy Świat

Zamoyski Palace on ul. Foksal

extremely high cost of restoring its Art Nouveau appearance. The street suffered from the newly nationalised economy that was unsuited to the commerce that characterised ul. Nowy Świat until 1939. Since the fall of communism, most shops have preferred to operate in shopping malls that offer larger, better-designed premises and parking for customers. So Nowy Świat has found a new niche: it is now home to many restaurants, with more opening almost every month. From May to September the street is closed to all traffic at weekends (during the week it is only open to buses and taxis) and the restaurants offer outdoor seating. There are still a good number of shops, mainly small boutique-style operations.

Ulica Foksal

Ulica Foksal runs off Nowy Świat and takes its name from Vauxhall Park in London, which inspired the creation of Foksal Park ('Foksal' is the Polish pronunciation of Vauxhall). The street leads down to the Leandro Marconi-designed **Zamoyski Palace**. There are a couple of other interesting palaces at the end of the street, one of which houses a very decent restaurant, **Villa Foksal** (*at No 3/5; tel: 022 827 8716*), but now the street is best known for the bars and clubs that line the section nearest Nowy Świat.

Ulica Kubusia Puchatka

Running parallel to Nowy Świat is ul. Kubusia Puchatka, quite literally 'Winnie the Pooh Street'. It's possibly the quietest street in the city as it leads nowhere and has no shops, just one (rather good) café. To make people back home believe you've walked down Winnie the Pooh Street, you must take a photograph of the street's nameplate: it shows a picture of Pooh and Piglet.

Aleje Ujazdowskie

Aleje Ujazdowskie continues the royal route heading south towards **Wilanów Palace** from the Royal Castle on pl. Zamkowy. Although extensively damaged in World War II, the vast majority of its palaces were rebuilt and the street is now known as 'embassy row' due to all the embassies either on it or close to it.

Plac Trzech Krzyży

Aleje Ujazdowskie starts in pl. Trzech Krzyży (Three Crosses Square), known to most expats as pl. Trzech because Trzech Krzyży is a bit of a tongue-twister. Much of the middle of the square is taken up by **St Alexander's Church**, built in 1818 and designed by Chrystian Piotr Aigner in his beloved neoclassical style. The square originally took its name from the church but is now named after the three crosses in the square: one on top of the church and two freestanding crosses that face the entrance to the church. Other notable structures on the square include the neo-Renaissance-style

The US Embassy

EMBASSY OF THE UNITED STATES OF AMERICA

That gorgeous al. Ujazdowskie contains a monstrosity like the US Embassy (*No 31*) puzzles many visitors. Once a stunning 19th-century Italian-designed palace stood there. In 1900 the palace was bought by the Czetwertyński family and survived the war. The communist government requisitioned the building but paid the Czetwertyńskis rent for it. In 1949 the property passed to Stanisław Czetwertyński, and by then the US government wanted to buy the site but he refused to sell. In 1954 Stanisław, who once worked for the USA for six weeks buying potatoes in 1947, was accused of being an American spy, thrown in prison and his property seized. While he was in prison, the US government bought the palace and tore it down. In its place is Warsaw's ugliest building (and there's a lot of competition for that title). Since the mid-1990s the Czetwertyński family have been trying to get compensation, but there is a clause in the lease signed in 1956 where Poland promises to 'free the United States of America from all claims to the property made in Polish courts by third parties', so no compensation can come from the USA. Instead, the family are fighting a long claim through the Polish courts for compensation from the Polish government.

Institute for the Deaf that dates from 1827. It is one of the world's oldest schools for the deaf and has a wonderful musical clock that, according to some, is supposed to remind people of the gift of hearing. The recently constructed neo-Renaissance style **Dom Dochodowy** (*pl. Trzech Krzyży 3*) is reputedly Warsaw's most expensive and arguably most beautiful office building. The square also contains a monument to Wincenty Witos. On 10

St Alexander's Church on pl. Trzech Krzyży

May 1926 a military coup led by Józef Piłsudski (*see p12*) removed Witos from office; he was the last democratically elected prime minister of Poland until Tadeusz Mazowiecki became the first prime minister of the Third Republic on 24 August 1989.

Parliament Building

Designed in 1925 and located just off al. Ujazdowskie at ul. Wiejska 2/4/6, this is one of Kazimierz Skorewicz's last and most famous buildings. Burnt to the ground in 1939 by the invading Nazi army, it was rebuilt to house the communist-era parliament, which had only one chamber and a rubber stamp to apply to the decisions of its leaders. The lack of a second chamber caused considerable problems in 1989 when the current system of a *Sejm* (lower house) and a *Senat* (upper house) was introduced.

Wilhelm Ellis Rau Palace

Next door to the US Embassy (*see box opposite*) is a delightful little palace called the Wilhelm Ellis Rau Palace. It was designed in 1866 by Leandro Marconi, who also designed the Great Synagogue on pl. Bankowy (*see p62*) – now sadly all gone apart from a small

piece of a stone column and a cloakroom ticket – and the Bristol Hotel (*see pp85–6*). The palace was originally in the neo-Renaissance style – one of Warsaw's first neo-Renaissance structures – but suffered extensive fire damage in 1944 and was rebuilt in 1948–9 to a more neoclassical design. Since then it has been the Swiss Embassy in Poland. Fortunately, the beautiful decorations on the side of the building, added in 1882 by Ludwik Kucharzewski, were preserved.
Aleje Ujazdowskie 27.

Ujazdowski Park

Another of Warsaw's firsts can be found in Ujazdowski Park, diagonally opposite the Wilhelm Ellis Rau Palace. The bridge here is Poland's first reinforced concrete structure. It dates back to 1898 and was designed by English engineer William Lindley, who was also responsible for Warsaw's water filtration plant. For more details about the park, *see p97.*

Ujazdowski Castle

The castle that gives al. Ujazdowskie its name is located on the other side of pl. Na Rozdrożu and Trasa Łazienkowska (*see p97*) from Ujazdowski Park. Badly damaged by Lithuanian troops in 1281, for 250 years the castle was largely ignored in favour of what is now the Royal Castle on pl. Zamkowy. The first stone structure on the site was built in 1548 at the order of Queen Bona Sforza, although it was only a small

residence. After being significantly enlarged in 1624, it was destroyed by the Swedish army in 1655 and rebuilt by Tylman van Gameren (also responsible for Krasińskich Palace, *see pp56–7*) in the Baroque style that can be seen today. After being given to the city of Warsaw in 1784, it served as a military hospital in World War I and then was razed to the ground in 1944, with only the exterior walls surviving. These walls were pulled down in 1953 because the site was earmarked for the culture centre of the Polish People's Army (fortunately never built). Rebuilding work started in 1975 and was completed in 1988. The castle now houses the CSW Modern Art Centre (*see p124*) and its terrace has an excellent view down the ornamental Royal Canal.
Aleje Ujazdowskie 6.

Prime Minister's Office

Last stop on al. Ujazdowskie is the Chancellery of the Chairman of the Council of Ministers (its official title) at No 1. Built in 1900, the building was at first home to the Field Marshal Aleksandr Suvorov Russian Military Academy. After World War I this military use continued; between 1920 and 1926 the building housed the Polish Infantry Academy, and from 1926 to 1939 it was the office of the General Inspectorate of the Armed Forces. In 1997 it became the Prime Minister's Office and has been a magnet for protests ever since.

Fryderyk Chopin Memorial

Fryderyk Chopin

Few figures in history come as close to defining the Romantic Age as pianist and composer Fryderyk Chopin (1810–49). Although much of his fame and reputation was earned while exiled abroad, he remains a Polish icon inexorably linked to Warsaw, and his presence and influence remain ingrained in both the Polish culture and psyche.

Born to French/Polish parents in the village of Żelazowa Wola, 50km (31 miles) from Warsaw (*see p140*), the family relocated to the capital a year later. Home-schooled in his early years, Chopin first started learning piano at the age of four, and it wasn't long before his talent was known to eminent musicians and landed gentry alike. A trip to the Fryderyk Chopin Museum reveals a gold watch given to the ten-year-old Chopin by a visiting Italian singer, while another exhibit recalls how he performed at the Presidential Palace at the age of eight in front of an audience that included the Tsar's brother. All true enthusiasts will want to visit this museum, and take a chronological tour of Chopin's life and times, including his teenage years spent studying at Warsaw's Lyceum, and his days spent in Parisian exile. The minutiae of his life have all been well preserved, from cuff links to letters, and even the last piano in his possession.

The Chopin family moved across Warsaw, at one time housed in the Saski Palace – where his father was a French tutor – as well as the Kazimierzowski Palace, in what is now a building of Warsaw University. Visitors won't find anything there connected to Chopin, but you will fare better by visiting another of his childhood homes at ul. Krakowskie Przedmieście 5, now converted into a museum. Although this residence was obliterated during World War II, it has since been restored, with a faithful re-creation of Chopin's drawing room – the highlight.

Chopin graduated in 1829, by which time he had already performed

The Fryderyk Chopin Museum

The manor and park in Żelazowa Wola where Chopin was born

several of his own compositions and been hailed as 'a musical genius' by one of his tutors. He set off to tour Europe in November 1830, but in the same month Poland rose in rebellion against the ruling Russians. Dissuaded from joining the uprising, he chose a life in exile, basing himself in Paris alongside other Polish émigrés such as the uncrowned king of Poland and the legendary bard Adam Mickiewicz.

Chopin's roots remained true in his Polkas and Mazurkas, and his compositions wooed Parisian audiences and catapulted him to international stardom. Moving in celebrity circles he met scandalous author George Sand in 1837 and embarked on a doomed love affair that would leave him heartbroken. When Sand published her novel *Lucrezia Floriani* in 1846, Chopin was commonly perceived as being the sickly anti-hero, and their turbulent relationship came to an end. Plagued by tuberculosis, Chopin passed away

in his apartment three years later, a broken shell of a man. His funeral was held on 30 October 1849 and was attended by thousands, with his body buried in Paris's Père-Lachaise Cemetery. Chopin was horrified at the prospect of being buried alive, so his heart was removed from his body and placed in an urn. Today this can be found interred inside a pillar in Warsaw's **Holy Cross Church** (*ul. Krakowskie Przedmieście 3*). He remains one of Warsaw's enduring heroes, and recitals of his work can be heard each summer by the Art Deco **Chopin Memorial** in Royal Łazienki Park every Sunday at noon and 4pm.

Fryderyk Chopin Museum: ul. Okólnik 1 (enter via ul. Tamka). Tel: 022 827 5473. Open: daily noon–8pm. Admission charge.

Chopin family home: ul. Krakowskie Przedmieście 5. Tel: 022 826 6251 ext 275. Open: 10am–6pm. Closed: Sat & Sun. Admission charge (except on Wed).

Parks

Despite its reputation as a rather grey city, Warsaw actually has a very good selection of green areas that can be enjoyed by visitors and Varsovians alike to enjoy. As well as the two forests that border the city, the Kampinos National Park (Kampinowski Park Narodowy) to the north and the Kabacki forest to the south, the city offers numerous parks of various sizes in which you can rest and relax or engage in more active pursuits.

Along the scarp that marks the eastern edge of the left side of the city is a series of parks that runs almost uninterrupted for several kilometres. From north to south they are: Kultury Park, Rydza-Śmigłego Park, Ujazdowski Park, Agrykola Park and the Royal Łazienki Park.

Those of Warsaw's parks that are fenced are generally open during hours of daylight, and those that are always open aren't places in which to loiter at night.

A peacock struts in Royal Łazienki Park

Kultury Park

Kultury Park is next to the National Museum (*see p126*) and the Military Museum. It runs alongside al. Jerozolimskie and also Most Poniatowskiego (Poniatowski Bridge). The bridge is the best way to get to the park – go down the metal stairs and the park is on your right as you face the river. The park has a good selection of paths where you can stroll in the shade of trees or just sit on one of the benches and relax. In the summertime there is a small bar at the corner of ul. Książęca and ul. Rozbrat, which is ideal for a cold beer or two and feeding bits of bread to the ducks on the nearby pond.
al. Jerozolimskie.

Rydza-Śmigłego Park

Rydza-Śmigłego Park is the other side of ul. Książęca from Kultury Park. Because the road slopes steeply here, the best way to get from one park to the other is the footbridge at the end of

A kiosk selling beer and ice cream in Agrykola Park

al. Na Skarpie. This park takes its name from Edward Rydz-Śmigły, Marshal of Poland from 1936 onwards. It sounds impressive but means he was a leader of the military dictatorship at the time when anti-Jewish laws were passed.

One of the features of the park is its bike trail and skate park, both popular with bladers and skaters. More sedate pleasures can be found at the outdoor bars that serve decent beer and simple but reasonably priced food.
al. Na Skarpie.

Ujazdowski Park

Covering approximately 5.7ha (14 acres), Ujazdowski Park is to the southwest of Rydza-Śmigłego Park. Ulica Piękna takes you between the two. Located moments from the hustle and bustle of pl. Trzech Krzyży, the park is an ideal place to rest and relax by strolling around the lake before

throwing yourself back on the tourist trail. Created in 1893–6, it was designed by Franciszek Szanior. Among the park's attractions is a weighing machine built in Lublin in 1898. After being exhibited at the Paris exposition of 1905 alongside the Eiffel Tower, the machine has been in the park since 1913. For a small fee, the machine operator will weigh you, and for a larger one they will lie about the result.
Corner of al. Ujazdowskie and ul. Piękna.

Agrykola Park

Between Agrykola and Ujazdowski parks is a six-lane highway called the Trasa Łazienkowska, which replaced earlier, smaller roads. Warsaw has neither a ring road nor an orbital highway. Instead, the main east–west road in Europe passes between two idyllic parks – not the greatest bit of planning by the communist government of the 1960s.

The lake in Ujazdowski Park

Somewhat confusingly, Agrykola Park, not Ujazdowski Park, is where you'll find Ujazdowski Castle (*see p92*). The castle now houses the CSW Modern Art Centre (*see p124*) and the **Qchnia Artystyczna** restaurant (*tel: 022 625 7627*). Unlike their neighbours in Royal Łazienki and Ujazdowski, the park-keepers in Agrykola are quite happy to allow picnicking, so if you've brought lunch, this is the place to eat it.

Royal Łazienki Park

Royal Łazienki Park and Agrykola Park are divided by a rarely used but rather steep road, ul. Agrykola. *See pp100–101 for a walk around Łazienki Park.*

Pole Mokotowskie

Pole Mokotowskie (Mokotów Field) is found in the Mokotów district to the south of the city centre and is vast, more than 61ha (150 acres). To give some sense of the scale, during the interwar years the park contained Warsaw airport (which was moved to its current location at Okęcie in 1934), a Polish air force base, a runway for aircraft, the aeronautical division of Warsaw Polytechnic, and the Warsaw horserace track, and still had room for plenty of public space! After suffering considerable damage during World War II, the park then suffered a renovation in the 1970s designed to show how great communism can be. The bizarre concrete pod-like structure that was part of the project is still baffling people today. On the plus side, the lake was enlarged, but don't be tempted to swim in it. During communist times part of the park also became the site of the Polish National Library.

The only real problem with Pole Mokotowskie is that it's too popular and can become very crowded, especially during weekends in the summer. Part of the reason for its popularity is the large number of concerts and shows organised here in summer. Another reason is the number of places selling good beer and any kind of food you want (provided you want meat that has been charred on a barbecue). Pick of the bunch, and a firm summer favourite with Varsovian expats, is Lolek (*see p165*).

Krasińskich Park

Not the biggest of parks but certainly one of the quieter ones. This park was once the private gardens of Krasińskich Palace (*see pp56–7*) but has been open to the public since 1768, four years after the Polish state purchased the palace. There's a decent-sized pond and a small spring that floods the path beneath it every time the rain's a little heavy. The southern corner of the park is where you'll find Warsaw's Arsenal (*see p70*).

Praski Park

Home to Warsaw Zoo (*see p153*), Praski Park covers some 70ha (173 acres) of Praga (the name translates as the 'Park in Praga') in right-bank Warsaw. If you're not a fan of staring at caged animals, take a stroll along the bench-lined paths that criss-cross the park.

Ujazdowski Castle within Agrykola Park

Walk: Royal Łazienki Park

Warsaw's biggest park, Royal Łazienki is an inner-city sanctum criss-crossed with walking trails, landscaped gardens, 18th-century architecture and a plethora of cafés.

This route, starting at the Chopin Memorial in the park (see pp64–5), takes in the main sights of the park, but do wander down any paths that take your fancy. There's plenty to see here – keep an eye out for red squirrels and peacocks.

Allow 2 hours.

1 Old Orangery

Having taken in the Chopin Memorial and walked past the Greek-influenced Temple of Diana, visitors find themselves faced with an 18th-century orangery, home to a collection of plant life, a sculpture gallery filled with pieces taken from King Stanisław Augustus Poniatowski's private collection, and the Stanisławowski Theatre, an imperial court theatre completed in 1777.

2 Biały Domek

Finished in 1777, this is an Italianesque villa built to resemble an inkstand. It had a simple purpose – a love nest in which the king could conduct his extramarital affairs. In 1801 it served as the home of Louis XVIII during his stay in Poland.

3 Palace on the Water

Once an ancient hunting ground for the Dukes of Mazovia, the area spanned by the Palace on the Water (or Łazienki Palace) was taken over in 1674 by the Lubomirski family, who commissioned

Tylman van Gameren to build a palace. It underwent a grand remodelling a century later when Dominik Merlini was brought in by the king to convert it into a summer retreat. Set on an artificial lake, the palace is connected to the rest of the park by two bridges and serves as a superb example of 18th-century Polish classical architecture. Sections now open to the public include an extravagant ballroom, royal living

The Palace on the Water

quarter, a bathhouse, portrait galleries and the Thursday Dinner Room, in which King Poniatowski held some of his occasionally bawdy gatherings with the prominent writers, artists and social luminaries of the day.

4 Myślewicki Palace

This grand white building was built in 1784 for the king's nephew, Józef Poniatowski, and his initials can still be seen engraved over the central window. Later it served as a military school, and it was the cadets and officers from this school who attacked the **Belweder Palace** in 1830 and sparked the November Uprising. Nowadays, it is home to the Paderewski Museum of Polish Emigration.

5 Theatre on the Island

Inspired by Herculaneum's amphitheatre, the Theatre on the Island was designed by J C Kamsetzer and opened in 1791. Penned in by trees, and with a canal separating the stage from the audience, this is a great spot to take in one of the performances held here each summer.

6 New Orangery

Conclude your walk at the New Orangery, made of cast iron and glass. The restaurant inside (*The Belvedere; tel: 022 841 2250*) is one of the most exclusive in the city: past guests include Hillary Clinton and Queen Elizabeth II. In summer dine outside while peacocks strut between the tables.

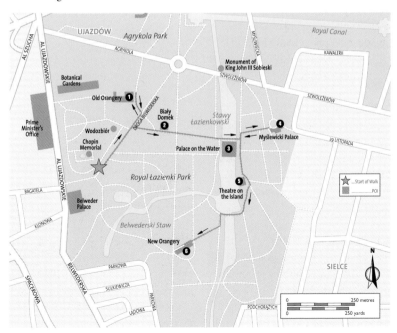

Socialist-realist Warsaw

If you were a Soviet architect in 1945, Warsaw was like all of your Christmases coming at once (not that you celebrated Christmas, of course): a ruined city to play with, a good budget and the instructions 'Make it impressive'. To give credit where it's due, the architects did leave behind some superb examples of socialist realism.

Most impressive is the Palace of Culture and Science (*see pp30–31*), but there are other examples

Massive streetlights on pl. Konstytucji

throughout the city. The best known of these is the MDM, *Marszałkowska Dzielnica Mieszkaniowa* (the Marszałkowska residential district). This development was built as part of the devious scheme of the post-war leaders who wanted to establish a communist centre in the old heart of capitalist Warsaw, where the 'bourgeoisie was rife'. The master plan was for huge parades to start from the Palace of Culture and Science, head down ul. Marszałkowska (which was widened so it would look more impressive), and then finish in pl. Konstytucji, where there would be rousing speeches by the leaders, and people could see the kind of housing 'good workers' could have. So out came the bulldozers and down went the buildings that had survived the war. The scale of the buildings on pl. Konstytucji is completely wrong: they are built to look good, not to be good to live in; almost every apartment has one or two rooms with no windows. However, the square does have three huge street lights that are best described as neo-Baroque candelabras on steroids.

Along ul. Marszałkowska between pl. Konstytucji and pl. Zbawiciela are

Tribute to the working man

some excellent reliefs that show eight model workers, each carrying the tools of their trade. These are perhaps the finest examples of socialist realism you'll find anywhere in Poland. Each figure shows a good, strong, honest member of the proletariat and glorifies the efforts he or she makes to advance the cause of socialism. Most people just look at the figures and say something along the lines of, 'Look at the size of his hands! They're like shovels!'

Head up ul. Marszałkowska to pl. Bankowy and then straight up ul. Andersa to the corner with ul. Stawki, and you'll find another, less well-known, showcase development. Two huge blocks, mirror images of each other, line the road back down towards ul. Anielewicza. Supposedly the plan was that such structures should line the length of ul. Andersa and ul. Marszałkowska all the way to the Palace of Culture and Science, but like so many great plans in Warsaw, it is still not finished and probably never will be.

Putting the 'real' into socialist realism in Warsaw is the Soviet Military Cemetery in Ochota (*ul. Żwirki i Wigury*). Built by Varsovians as an entirely spontaneous gesture of their thanks at being liberated and their desire not to visit Siberia, the place is on a truly epic scale and looks even bigger because it is always deserted. A trip there is half worthwhile just to see the figures in the relief. This features the liberating Red Army being welcomed by Poles who look remarkably well fed and are good, honest workers. The little girl on the left of the left-hand relief is not a worker but instead a miracle worker: she's found fresh tulips in bombed-out Warsaw in the middle of January. The gentleman next but one to her is officially being given a Red Flag by a Soviet soldier, but when the shadows are right he appears to be having his coat stolen.

Central Warsaw

There are two areas of particular interest in this part of the city. Ulica Marszałkowska runs from pl. Unii Lubelskiej north to pl. Bankowy. Due to its status as the main street in Warsaw it received particular attention from communist-era planners, with predictably dire results.

Aleje Jerozolimskie was once one of the wealthiest streets in Warsaw and, despite wartime destruction, still retains much of interest today.

Ulica Marszałkowska

First built in 1757 as the main road for the Bielino development, established by Grand Marshal Franciszek Bieliński, for the first 13 years of its existence the street was called ul. Bielińska before changing to its current name. As the street gained importance, the original wooden houses were replaced with ever more grandiose structures and tenement houses up to six storeys high. By 1918 it had become the favourite street for large companies to locate their head offices. Many of its buildings were destroyed during World War II and very few were rebuilt in their original form.

The obvious place to start is the tram stop where pl. Unii Lubelskiej meets Marszałkowska. From there, either walk or take the tram up the street to pl. Zbawiciela. This section of the street has been rebuilt in varying degrees of socialist-realist severity and has the feel of a somewhat run-down Parisian neighbourhood, but without the vibrant immigrant community. Plac Zbawiciela is a very pleasant place (*see pp112–13*), and ul. Marszałkowska leaves pl. Zbawiciela and heads up into the MDM development towards pl. Konstytucji (*see p102*). No matter how lazy you're feeling, get off the tram at pl. Zbawiciela and walk up to pl. Konstytucji: neither the socialist-realist sculptures of the working man and woman along Marszałkowska nor the bizarre streetlights on pl. Konstytucji should be missed.

Next stop (assuming you can avoid the rather good cake shop on the left-hand side as you leave pl. Konstytucji) is ul. Wilcza. This street marks the end of the MDM development, hence the monumental architecture of buildings on both of the southern corners, and is worth a stroll both for the surviving pre-war buildings and the decent bars at the corner of Wilcza and Poznanska (Kwadrat and Warsaw Tortilla Factory) and at Wilcza No 23 (Lodi Dodi). From here, walk up to Marszałkowska No 72, the Matias Taubenhaus residence, a very impressive neo-Gothic pile designed by Edward Goldberg and built in 1898.

From here, jump on a tram, head up the street past the Eastern Wall development (*see pp108–9*) and get off at ul. Świętokrzyska. Turn right into ul. Świętokrzyska and walk down to the corner with pl. Powstańców Warszawy. What is now the Hotel Warszawa (*No 9*) used to be a superb Art Deco building housing the offices of the Prudential Insurance company and, at 18 storeys high, it was the first skyscraper in Warsaw. Its steel skeleton gave it sufficient strength to survive intense Nazi bombardment, although much of the stone was blown away.

Unfortunately, it was rebuilt along socialist-realist lines and is a pale shadow of its former self. Directly opposite the hotel is the astoundingly ugly **Polish National Bank building**, nicknamed *trumna* (the coffin). Recover from the trauma of seeing it by turning right off pl. Powstańców Warszawy into ul. Szpitalna and walking down to the Wedel chocolate shop (*ul. Szpitalna 8*) for a cup of the finest hot chocolate in the country.

Aleje Jerozolimskie

The name of Jerozolimskie can be traced to 1774 and Nowa Jerozolima, a village populated mainly by Jews. The construction of Warsaw's first train station proved a shot in the arm for the

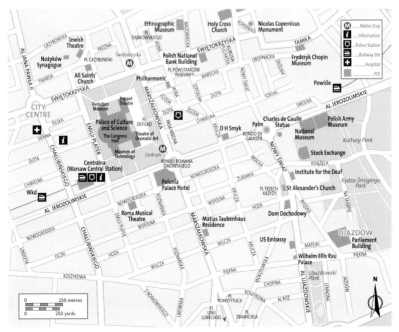

district. Many of the Art Nouveau structures which dominated the area fell victim to the war, but the street still retains its importance.

Charles de Gaulle Statue

Since 2005 a statue of Charles de Gaulle has stood looking out towards the roundabout named after him: Rondo de Gaulle'a. But why? De Gaulle actually lived in Warsaw during the 1920s, and in 1920 he fought so heroically against the Bolsheviks in the Battle of Warsaw that he was awarded Poland's highest military honour: the Virtuti Militari. It's commonly accepted by historians that Poland's success against the invading Soviets saved western Europe from communism, and de Gaulle's contribution has not been forgotten.

D H Smyk

The D H Smyk children's department store is on the corner of ul. Krucza and al. Jerozolimskie. Opened in 1952, this glass-and-concrete novelty is a superb example of functionalism, with a design that was originally intended to evoke comparisons to a 'glowing lantern'. It does no such thing, or certainly not since a fire ravaged the original details back in the 1970s. Its current owners, DTC Real Estate, are looking to restore D H Smyk to its former glory.

ul. Krucza 50 (corner of al. Jerozolimskie).

The Matias Taubenhaus residence

Greetings from Jerusalem, Warsaw's palm tree

Palm

You wouldn't normally associate palm trees with Poland, but that's what you'll find standing on Rondo de Gaulle'a (*corner of al. Jerozolimskie and ul. Nowy Świat*). Erected in 2002 after a year of lobbying city authorities for planning permission, the palm is the work of Joanna Rajkowska. Inspired by a trip to Israel, the installation is officially titled *Greetings from Jerusalem* and is actually no more than a bendy steel column sprinkled with natural bark and fake leaves.

Polonia Palace Hotel

Founded by a family of aristocrats, the Polonia Palace originally opened in 1913. It was the first hotel in Warsaw to feature running water in each room and a modern central heating system. The interwar years marked a golden age for the hotel and it became known as a celebrity haunt. It escaped World War II unscathed, with General Eisenhower hosting a victory banquet here in 1945, and many ambassadors took up residence in the immediate aftermath of the war. After years operating as a glum state-run hotel, the Polonia Palace has once more resumed its position as one of Warsaw's most luxurious hotels.
al. Jerozolimskie 45.

Warsaw Central Station

Warsaw Central Station hasn't always been considered an eyesore; when it was completed in 1975 it was so futuristic that rural Poles demanded the opportunity to be bussed in from across Poland to admire the station and take guided tours of it. Built to coincide with Brezhnev's visit to Warsaw, a special entrance was constructed for him, and features included Poland's first moving ramp as well as the first escalator to be built in the country. Now grubby and generally hideous, the station is, if nothing else, a reminder of Poland's communist heritage.

The Eastern Wall

Running along the eastern side of ul. Marszałkowska between the corners with al. Jerozolimskie and ul. Świętokrzyska is a development called Ściana Wschodnia (the Eastern Wall): buildings that are bad even by the standards of communist-era architecture. So bad that it's worth having a look.

Post-World War II, this area was covered mainly by ruins and temporary buildings; people removing the rubble had been paid per cubic metre shifted and they'd been a little over-enthusiastic. In 1958 a contest was held for Polish architects to submit their concepts for the redevelopment. Winner Zbigniew Karpiński (the architect responsible for the US Embassy on ul. Piękna) was appointed general designer and in 1960 set to work with a team of experts to create the master plan.

Construction started in 1962 and was completed in 1969. The development consists of 23 buildings with a total volume of 680,000sq m (7,316,000sq ft). At the time it was considered state of the art: all three of Poland's tallest residential buildings (24 storeys each) were part of the project, along with eight 11-storey blocks. Other structures included four department stores (Wars, Sawa, Junior and Sezam), an office block called Universal, the Relax cinema, a pedestrian walkway named Pasa Wiecha, and the Rotunda, a circular bank. Social elements included cafés, a theatre, a couple of bars and, daringly, a nightclub.

First to run into serious trouble was the Rotunda: at 12.40pm on 15 February 1979, it exploded into a mass of tangled metal and glass shards; debris and banknotes lined ul. Marszałkowska and al. Jerozolimskie. Forty-five people died in the building and a further four in hospital; seventy-seven more were injured. Rumour said the explosion was a terrorist attack. Conspiracy theorists claimed rogue elements of the secret police had blown up the building to cover up their robbing the bank. Suspicion was heightened when the official explanation was a gas leak: the building had no gas. However, gas had leaked from pipes 8m (26ft) away from the bank and up a telecommunications channel into the bank. The bank was rebuilt at high speed, reopening in November 1979, and a plaque commemorates the dead.

Martial Law saw the department stores empty of everything except

The Eastern Wall in the 1970s

queues, and the early years of capitalism weren't much kinder: the nightclub became a stripclub of ill repute; the best bar became a fast-food outlet; and the department stores discovered that in the free market it's not good to have staff who view customers as vermin and stock as something to be hoarded. The downward spiral continued for more than a decade before investors were found and Wars, Sawa and Junior were almost entirely reconstructed, with Wars and Sawa becoming Galeria Centrum. Pasa Wiecha recently underwent much heralded renovation work but that seems to have been limited to new paving, bizarre massive streetlights

and washing 35 years' worth of grime off the walls. Apartments in the high-rise buildings are very difficult to sell, and the Universal building, once the office location of choice in Warsaw, has become little more than the world's largest permanent billboard.

If you want to see what Ściana Wschodnia was like back in the day, your best bet is Sezam. It's still in its original form (minus the parts that have fallen off) and features a shopping experience like the original one. When leaving, make sure you have a look at the greenhouse-like structure at the end of Sezam: it was the first McDonald's outlet to open in Poland.

Walk: South-central Warsaw

The area just to the south of pl. Konstytucji is a curious mix of pre-war tenement buildings and more recent low-rise blocks. Residential buildings mingle with offices and small shops occupy lower levels. The jumble of periods makes it an interesting area to explore and there are some real architectural treasures to discover.

Start at Politechnika Metro Station for ul. Polna.

Allow 2 hours.

1 Ulica Polna

As soon as you walk down ul. Polna, the contrasts of the area become apparent. On the left-hand side is a shiny new office block, while on the right-hand side stand old, less cared for apartment buildings with peeling

Warsaw Polytechnic's Aula

paintwork. Further along is a well-known market that has been operating since the 1950s. During communism, when a wide range of goods was unavailable, those who had money (preferably dollars) would come to the Polna market and buy products that could not be found elsewhere. There was always fruit, meat and chocolate here; hence Varsovians nicknamed Polna market the 'Delicatessen of Warsaw'. In the late 1990s the traditional open-air market moved into a modern building, with the stalls spread over two levels. This still provides Varsovians with fresh, high-quality but rather highly priced products.

Go along ul. Polna to pl. Politechniki.

2 Warsaw Polytechnic

Warsaw Polytechnic is housed in several buildings spread across the city, the most impressive of which is the main building at pl. Politechniki. Completed in 1901, the structure is pentagon-shaped, designed by Stefan Szyller, and a neo-Renaissance masterpiece. It features a large glass roof soaring four storeys above a courtyard ringed with three galleries. The Baroque-influenced staircase is quite simply stunning. The courtyard is known as the Aula (Assembly Hall); unsurprisingly, it is hired out for concerts and all manner of events – it has even hosted the Miss World competition. The building also contains a library, academic offices and smaller lecture rooms. The front of the building is attractively decorated and features a relief above the main entrance that clearly doffs its cap to science.

Walk up ul. Lwowska.

3 Ulica Lwowska

This is one of five streets that run off pl. Politechniki and it contains many turn-of-the-twentieth-century buildings that escaped destruction during World War II. Ulica Śniadeckich, one street across, is also worth a look for its architecture, but the buildings on ul. Lwowska are among the most impressive in the area. Be sure to look up: the most decorative stonework and ornate ironwork are found towards the roofs. The buildings at Nos 15 and 17 are particularly impressive, and the courtyard at No 13 even houses a tiny palace dating from 1912. On the corner with ul. Koszykowa stands what was once the

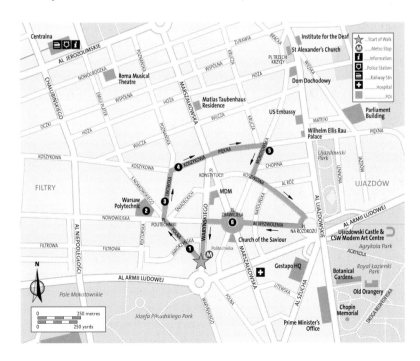

Russian college and is now Warsaw Polytechnic's architecture department. *Walk the length of ul. Lwowska and turn right into ul. Koszykowa.*

4 Ulica Koszykowa

Koszykowa is a real mixture: some parts are falling to pieces and house ancient small businesses; other parts are the domain of modern office space and thoroughly renovated. It is worth taking a stroll down: walk along ul. Koszykowa into pl. Konstytucji, go straight across and you're in ul. Piękna, which literally means 'Beautiful Street'. Thanks to the post-war planners, ul. Koszykowa leaves pl. Konstytucji from the bottom right-hand corner. Ulica Piękna is a real jumble of styles, with modern structures next to, and sometimes surrounding, older buildings. Some of the older buildings appear to be held together by steel rods and the power of prayer.

From ul. Piękna, turn right into ul. Mokotowska.

5 Ulica Mokotowska and Aleje Wyzwolenia

The first crossroads along ul. Piękna is ul. Mokotowska, which runs from pl. Trzech Krzyży, across pl. Zbawiciela and down to ul. Polna. Ulica Mokotowska has offices and residential buildings in various states of repair and some decent little restaurants. Beautifully restored pre-war constructions and gleaming glass-fronted modern offices stand next to buildings with crumbling brickwork and temporary wooden shelters or wire-mesh nets to protect pedestrians from falling masonry. Turn left down ul. Koszykowa and you'll reach pl. Na Rozdrożu; the first right takes you into al. Wyzwolenia. This is a much wider avenue than many of the streets in the area, primarily residential and lined with old leafy trees. It's part of the MDM development (*see p102*) and looks very much like a socialist-realist version of Place Vendôme in Paris.

From al. Wyzwolenia, walk to pl. Zbawiciela.

6 Plac Zbawiciela

Aleje Wyzwolenia takes you to pl. Zbawiciela, the heartland of the revival of south-central Warsaw. It's home to a painfully trendy café (Coffee Karma) infested with faux-bohemians, but there is a good sushi place (Izumi Sushi) if you're hungry and happy to pay PLN70+ per person. If that's too much for you, or you just fancy a lighter meal, pop into Bastylia (*ul. Mokotowska 17, on the corner with pl. Zbawiciela*) for the finest crêpes in Warsaw. Try the 'Italian' crêpe filled with minced meat, Bolognaise sauce and cheese (PLN15) or the nutella and banana crêpe (PLN9).

The six streets that come off the square fan out evenly, creating a convenient central meeting spot for the surrounding area. On the corner of Mokotowska across from Bastylia is the wonderfully eccentric building that houses the Methodist language school, for many years the only English language school in communist-era Warsaw.

By far the most beautiful building on pl. Zbawiciela is the **Church of the Saviour** (Kościół Zbawiciela). Although construction started in 1901, it was only consecrated in 1927 – due, in part, to World War I. An eclectic design that mixes Gothic, Renaissance and Baroque elements, inside, the church is rather less ornate than might be expected, but there are columns and arches that are echoed in the architecture around the square and beyond. Its gleaming white walls and twin spires are beautifully lit at night.

From pl. Zbawiciela, continue along ul. Nowowiejska and then left at al. Waryńskiego to get back to Politechnika Metro Station.

Church of the Saviour on pl. Zbawiciela

Monuments

Poland's turbulent past and roller-coaster existence have seen a fair share of its heroes step from the shadows and assume their place in history. All of these have been celebrated in stone, and while structures commemorating the likes of Chopin and Copernicus have been well documented, a number serve only to baffle the less informed visitor.

The Aviator

On the roundabout that marks the start of ul. Żwirki i Wigury stands a monument of a lone aviator, designed by Edward Wittig and originally placed on pl. Unii Lubelskiej in 1932. Demolished by the Nazis, it was reconstructed in 1967 before being positioned on its current site. Though it only depicts one man, the statue is dedicated to two: Franciszek Żwirko and Stanisław Wigura. The pair were Poland's most celebrated flying aces, clinching victory in the Challenge 1932 international air contest. National heroes, the pair died when their plane crashed in stormy weather.

Józef Piłsudski

Overlooking the square named after him, pl. Piłsudskiego, is a glum-looking Field Marshal Piłsudski, who spent five years locked up in Siberia accused of attempting to kill the tsar. He was later credited with winning Poland its independence in 1918, and successfully defending its borders from Bolshevik aggression years later.

Monte Cassino

The monument at ul. Długa 52 commemorates the contribution Polish troops made in the Battle of Monte Cassino. The Allied advance on Rome in 1944 had been thwarted by German resistance, and what should have been a speedy advance became bogged down in a siege that cost 25,000 lives. Polish troops stepped in and broke the deadlock, raising the Polish flag over the ruins of the Monte Cassino monastery on 18 May 1944. The road to Rome was open. The monument was erected in 1999 and unveiled on the 55th anniversary of the victory.

The Monument to Those Deported and Murdered in the East

Standing across from the Ibis Hotel on ul. Muranowska, this monument dates from 1995 and was designed by Max Biskupski. It features hundreds of crosses (and a few Jewish tombstones) piled on to a railway wagon, thereby commemorating the thousands of Poles who were deported to Siberia during the Stalinist era.

Nike

Just before reaching the Trasa W-Z Tunnel that runs underneath pl. Zamkowy, visitors can view a statue of Nike, the Greek goddess of victory. Nike stands on a sandstone plinth with her sword raised defiantly in the air. Officially named the 'Monument to the Heroes of Warsaw 1939–1945', this fearsome construction remembers the men and women of Warsaw who fought against German occupation. The statue was erected in 1964, originally on pl. Teatralny. At the time there was no official memorial to the Warsaw Uprising so Nike became a rallying point for veteran insurgents, and later for student dissidents. In 1999 the reconstruction of pl. Teatralny saw Nike hauled across to her current location.

Syrena

Incorporated in the city's coat of arms since 1622, the *syrena* (mermaid) is the symbol of Warsaw, and a statue of her wielding a sword and shield takes centre stage atop a fountain in the Old Town Market Square. According to popular legend, it was a mermaid that guided a lost prince, Kazimierz, to the site of what is now Warsaw, inspiring him to found the city. Two other statues honour her good work, on ul. Karowa and on Świętokrzyski Bridge.

The Monument to Those Deported and Murdered in the East

Praga

Praga was traditionally the 'wrong side of the river': frontier territory for thugs, malcontents and ne'er-do-wells. But the last 15 years have seen Praga claw its way up from an embarrassing no-go zone to a regeneration hotspot. Largely undamaged by World War II, many of Praga's streets retain their original architecture. Low rents once lured a raft of artists and beatniks to the area, while keeping many of the drunks and petty criminals as well. Is it sleazy or authentic? Fashionable or pretentious? Come and see.

Although Praga was officially incorporated into Warsaw in 1791, it was a few decades later that the area really began to develop, due mainly to the construction of the Wileńska railway station and the numerous red-brick factories that mushroomed around it. It was in the post-World War II years that the area acquired its nefarious reputation, largely thanks to the government policy of housing what they saw as undesirable elements in Praga's cramped tenement buildings. Today, as investment continues to roll in, there's a real expectancy among trend predictors for Praga to gradually transform into Warsaw's answer to New York's SoHo. Edgy, artsy and full of surprises, Praga is an immensely enjoyable day trip for those looking to explore the less vanilla side of Warsaw.

Bazar Różyckiego

With the Stadium Market (*see pp122–3*) looking almost certainly doomed,

Varsovians and tourists alike have turned their attention to Bazar Różyckiego to get their fill of dangerous electrical appliances, genuine fakes and similar items of debatable origin. In operation since 1901, and little larger than a football pitch, at first glance the market is every bit a caricature of modern-day Dickensian disaster: old women bent double selling turnips and shifty males pushing pirated goods. Yet for all the low-quality rubbish, great bargains are to be had, with many stalls selling fresh farm produce. It's also a good place for specialist souvenirs, such as old postcards and paraphernalia from the former Soviet Union. This market witnessed a dramatic decline after the creation of the Stadium Market, but as the grim reaper stalks the stadium, the future looks considerably brighter for Bazar Różyckiego, still regarded by many locals as Warsaw's original market. *ul. Ząbkowska. Open: Mon–Fri 6am–5pm, Sat 6am–3pm. Closed: Sun.*

Bear Island

What you didn't expect to see while eating top-end kebabs in Warsaw was three bears to plod past you, but that's exactly what you'll be faced with if you get a takeaway from Le Cedre, cross al. Solidarności and stand looking towards Praski Park. More than 400 bears have been reared on this concrete island since 1949, and the three current residents are a hands-down hit with children and adults alike. Although a deep moat keeps the bears at bay, this hasn't prevented the occasional drunk from paying them a visit in order to demonstrate who's boss; the current score is drunks nil, bears several.

al. Solidarności.

Cathedral of Saints Michael and Florian

In defiant retaliation to the construction of the nearby Orthodox Church, Father Ignacy Dutkiewicz campaigned for a new Catholic place of worship to service the people of Praga. The result was a fearsome cathedral crowned with a pair of steel-studded 75m (246ft) high steeples. Completed in 1902, the interiors are surprisingly austere considering the local propensity for ecclesiastical extravagance, although the photograph in the entrance will leave visitors in no doubt as to the size of the rebuilding project that followed World War II.

ul. Floriańska 3.

Praga

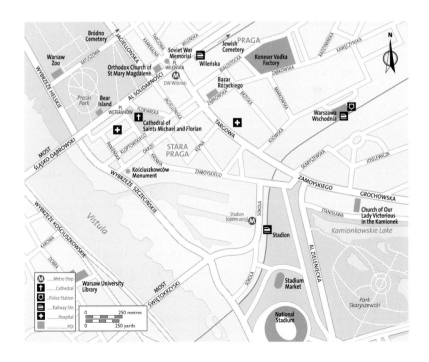

Jewish heritage

Pre-war Praga had a sizeable Jewish population and they left a scattering of sights. The house on ul. Targowa 50/52 used to be a synagogue, and although the building was turned into a warehouse after the war, faded wall paintings depicting the tomb of Rachel and the Western Wall can still be

discerned. Further afield, a visit to the **Jewish Cemetery** (*corner of ul. Św. Wincentego and ul. Odrowąża*) makes for a particularly moving afternoon. Founded in 1780, this was the burial ground for the impoverished. It was not spared the bile of the Nazis, with several tombs used to pave streets. Disturbingly, the post-war Polish

Orthodox Church of St Mary Magdalene

government sanctioned further destruction and the remaining tombstones were bulldozed and left in smashed piles of rubble. These can still be viewed today, and serve as a forlorn tribute to Warsaw's tragic past.

Koneser Vodka Factory

Clustered in a group of historical red-brick listed buildings, the Koneser Vodka Factory has been doing business since 1897, with end-products including Metropolis, Warszawska, Targowa and, of course, their signature distinguished brand, Koneser Vodka. The factory, a great example of the industrial architecture of the day, was the first in Warsaw to use electricity, and many original details such as the cast-iron roses that adorn the brickwork have been faithfully preserved. For many visitors appreciation of the exterior design plays second fiddle to the vodka tours the factory now offers. Pre-booked tours cost PLN25 (or PLN30 if you want to finish with a taste test), and take visitors all the way through the production process.
ul. Ząbkowska 27/31. Tel: 022 619 9021. Open: Daily for pre-booked tours. Admission charge (extra charge at weekends).

Orthodox Church of St Mary Magdalene

Featuring five onion domes and a lemon-yellow colour scheme, this church is a feast for the eyes. It has an equally elaborate interior that drips with frescoes and gold gilding. Completed in 1869 to a design by Mikołaj Syczew, this masterpiece took just two years to build. Its purpose was to serve the huge Russian-speaking population that at the time populated Tsarist-controlled Warsaw, particularly the Russian railway workers who lived nearby. A few of the mosaics now decorating the chapel originally came from the St Alexander Nevsky Cathedral, which once dominated what is now pl. Piłsudskiego and disappeared after Polish independence in 1918. The Orthodox Church of St Mary Magdalene was one of only two Orthodox churches left standing in Warsaw in 1939, and miraculously it survived World War II virtually intact.
al. Solidarności 52.

Soviet War Memorial

This is Warsaw's most maligned monument, so much so that it rarely appears in official tourist pamphlets and is often daubed with the artistic spray-painting of bored youths. The memorial commemorates the Soviet soldiers who died in the liberation of Poland. Although 600,000 Red Army soldiers were killed on Polish soil, bitter feelings of betrayal still linger. Though there are no plans to remove the monument (as happened recently in Estonia), its state of disrepair speaks volumes for the rancour with which the former Soviet Union is regarded. A popular local nickname for the monolith is the 'four sleepers', and not

only because of the dozy-looking cast-iron statues that stand on each corner of the base: Praga is where the Soviet war machine chose to cease its hitherto relentless advance, allowing western Warsaw to be devastated during the Warsaw Uprising (*see pp14–15*).
Corner of ul. Targowa and al. Solidarności.

Stara Praga (Old Praga)

Stara Praga covers the area penned in by Praski Park, the National Stadium and Warszawa Wschodnia Station. Its

A courtyard shrine in Praga

network of tight, shambolic streets is an intriguing mix of recently renovated town houses and the burnt-out ruins from either World War II or a recent gang turf war (most probably the former). To walk some of the streets is like stepping back in time; the area was considered sufficiently decrepit by film director Roman Polański to shoot several scenes from *The Pianist* here. Walk to ul. Wybrzeże Szczecińskie to view the fearsome-looking **Kościuszkowców Monument**, unveiled in 1985 to honour Polish troops who attempted to cross the Vistula River to relieve their comrades during the Warsaw Uprising.

Tollgate houses

A pair of tollgate houses stand opposite each other on ul. Grochowska. Designed in 1818 by Jakub Kubicki, the white classicist buildings are distinguished by their porches, bas reliefs and Greco-Roman columns. They were built at the beginning of ul. Brzeski leading into Warsaw (now Grochowska), opened in 1823, and the two structures were occupied by a police officer and a toll collector. Today, they have been fully restored and provide much-needed relief from the surrounding sepia blocks.
ul. Grochowska.

Ulica Ząbkowska

No other street captures the force of Praga's resurgence like Ząbkowska, the spiritual heartland of the theatrical

Ulica Ząbkowska: the heart of the Praga resurgence

types who have resettled in the area. Decades of neglect saw local inhabitants nickname the street 'Ruin Canyon', and it came within a whisker of being condemned for wholesale demolition in the 1990s. The dawn of the 21st century saw concerted efforts to restore the area, with astonishing results. Crumbling tenements have since been converted into luxurious apartments, while the 'everything for PLN5' shops have slowly been pushed out by galleries and atmospheric cafés filled with whispering academics. At the centre of this artsy revival is Łysy Pingwin (The Bald Penguin), a superb bar at ul. Ząbkowska 11. Head here to listen to unsigned DJs practising on the decks, impromptu poetry readings, and to see patrons playing *boules* in the backyard. The long-term aim, optimistic as it may seem, is to turn Ząbkowska into an attraction to rival anything Warsaw's west bank has to offer, with plans afoot to re-create the pre-war spirit.

Walk: Saska Kępa

Warsaw's other main right-bank neighbourhood, Saska Kępa is commonly regarded as Warsaw's most affluent area and has the detached atmosphere of an English village.

Start your walk at Poniatowski Bridge, then hopefully enjoy the brand new stadium before taking in Skaryszewski Park and a delightful modern church.

Allow 2 hours.

1 Most Poniatowskiego (Poniatowski Bridge)

Warsaw's best bridge carries visitors from the centre straight into Saska Kępa. Constructed at incredible cost between 1904 and 1914, the bridge has been bombed twice and dynamited once over the course of two wars. Adding to its woes, it was on this bridge that rebels announced their 1926 coup that ended Poland's last democratically elected government for 63 years. Nowadays, the bridge is back to its best after a programme of renovation saw its neo-Renaissance turrets and towers restored.

Make your way to the National Stadium, on your left as you reach the end of the bridge.

2 National Stadium

Quite what the site of the National Stadium will look like on your visit is anyone's guess. The former Tenth Anniversary Stadium was completed in 1955 – a showpiece of socialist-realist design and Polish ingenuity. It was built by piling up rubble from World War II in a bowl shape, topping that with concrete, fitting benches around the sides and planting grass in the middle. It was a cunning plan but one that led to the stadium being hopelessly outdated by the mid-1980s and all but abandoned. In 1989 Europe's largest outdoor market, and Poland's premier font of blackmarket goods, sprang up in and around the stadium. As a result of Poland being chosen to host Euro 2012, by 2011 you will hopefully see a sparkling new 55,000-seat stadium where the tournament's first match will be played (along with two group matches, a quarter-final and a semi-final). There should also be a 15,000-seat indoor arena, an Olympic-sized swimming pool with seats for 4,000 spectators, a hotel and a conference centre – over one billion złoty well spent, hopefully. There might even be the second Metro line! However, this is Poland, so expect the unexpected. If you're lucky, you'll still be able to find a few socialist-realist statues dotted around the edge of the new stadium. *Make your way past the stadium and towards Skaryszewski Park.*

3 Skaryszewski Park

Founded in 1905, Skaryszewski Park is a riveting tapestry of lakes, cycle paths and flowerbeds, interspersed with a number of interwar monuments, and one dedicated to the crew of a B-24 Allied bomber shot down over Warsaw while dropping supplies during the Warsaw Uprising. Although pleasant and family oriented during the day, exercise caution if visiting by yourself during later hours.

4 Kamionkowskie Lake

Kamionkowskie Lake marks the boundary between Saska Kępa and Praga, and has witnessed its share of historical drama. In 1572 the first elected king of Poland, Henri de Valois, was chosen here, while in the following century Swedish and Polish armies contested the Battle of Warsaw nearby. The Polish victory has since been immortalised in Henryk Sienkiewicz's trilogy *The Deluge.*
Return to ul. Waszyngtona and head down ul. Saska, to the Holy Mother of God and Constant Aid Church.

5 Holy Mother of God and Constant Aid Church

This is a modern church that takes your breath away on account of an interior

decorated with modernist mosaics. Construction originally started in 1938, but the outbreak of World War II meant that the church was only completed in 1956. A plaque remembers the soldiers who died while defending the suburb from the Germans in 1939.
Head down ul. Saska again, before turning right on Zwycięzców to reach ul. Francuska.

6 Ulica Francuska

Finish your walk by strolling up this tree-lined street. Ulica Francuska is Saska Kępa's main high street and is filled with small cafés and signposts pointing the way to gated embassy residences. It's also worth taking some time to explore a few of the side streets, many of which are home to some striking Art Deco villas.

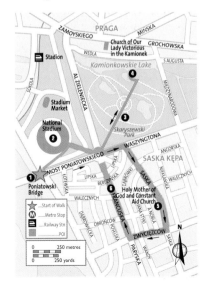

Museums and galleries

Warsaw has a rich array of museums and galleries, and to see them all would add several days to a visitor's itinerary. Aside from the museums already mentioned in this guidebook, the following represent the museum highlights of Warsaw, with the best of the bunch being the National Museum – a grand effort festooned with works from Europe's most prominent artists.

Those looking for more specific diversions will be pleased to learn that Warsaw has no shortage of eccentric museums, with separate ones dedicated to the fire brigade, technology and trains; there's even a **Gas Industry Museum** (*ul. Marcina Kasprzaka 25*). As befits a capital city, Warsaw has also acquired a reputation for being on the cutting edge of the Polish art scene, and this is reflected by the number of high-quality galleries showcasing the latest trends.

Most museums close one day a week, traditionally Monday, and most have one day a week when entrance is free. While the situation has improved radically, many museums can still be monolingual, and some also charge extra if you want to take any photographs inside the museum.

CSW Modern Art Centre

Founded in the 1980s, the CSW Modern Art Centre showcases contemporary, sometimes outrageous, art from across the world and much

much more. The exhibits are housed in a Baroque castle dating from 1730 (*see p92*), and the premises are also home to a slacker-style bar, a MoPo (Modern Polish, apparently) restaurant, a cinema, a library and a superb bookshop stocking a variety of art-related tomes. *Ujazdowski Castle, al. Ujazdowskie 6. Open: Tue–Thur, Sat & Sun noon–7pm, Fri noon–9pm. Closed: Mon. Admission charge except on Thur.*

Ethnographic Museum

Located in a neo-Renaissance residence designed by Enrico Marconi (*see p68*), the Ethnographic Museum contains a plethora of Polish folk costumes, art and handicrafts, as well as dioramas that illustrate the details of rustic life. Also on display are collections from Africa, Australia, Oceania, and Central and South America, including some wonderful tribal masks. *ul. Kredytowa 1. Open: Tue–Thur 10am–6pm, Fri 10am–4pm, Sat 10am–5pm, Sun noon–5pm. Closed:*

*Mon & holidays. Admission charge
except on Sat.*

Firemen's Museum

A favourite with pre-teen boys, although
seriously recommended for all ages, this
excellent museum recounts the story
of the Warsaw fire brigade from its
beginnings in 1836 right through to
the present day. Gaining access is an
adventure in itself, involving much
doorbell ringing before being ushered
into the 150-year-old depot. The
museum is a series of rooms featuring
gleaming fire engines, helmets, awards,
uniforms and fire-fighting equipment.
One hall features a collection of items
recovered from fires around Warsaw,
including computers, canisters and even
a piece of the passenger plane that
crashed just outside Warsaw in 1980,
killing 87 people.
*ul. Chłodna 3. Open: Mon–Fri
10am–2pm. Closed: Sat & Sun.
Free admission.*

Museum of Technology

A splendidly nonsensical museum
found deep inside the Palace of Culture
and Science. Lose yourself inside a

Zachęta Gallery

The main staircase in the Zachęta Gallery

labyrinth of rooms filled with a collection of contraptions that includes motorbikes, a virtual mine shaft, juke boxes, furnace doors and eight-bit Spectrum computers. Spaceship models, 1950s washing machines and a glass lady contribute to the madness. If nothing else, a trip to the Museum of Technology presents a thoroughly bizarre way to spend an afternoon.
pl. Defilad 1 (Pałac Kultury i Nauki, PKiN). Tel: 022 656 6759. Open: Tue–Fri 9am–5pm, Sat & Sun 10am–5pm. Closed: Mon. Admission charge.

National Museum

Founded in 1862 as the Museum of Fine Art, the National Museum has operated under its current name since 1916 and is home to one of the most important collections of artwork in Poland. Housed inside a blockish building dating from 1938, displays include a unique collection of 7th-

century Christian frescoes recovered from Sudan, as well as pre-war sculptures, works by Botticelli and 15th-century Dutch and Flemish paintings. Pride of place goes to the Polish modern art gallery with works from Poland's leading 20th-century artists: Majkowski, Malczewski and the wonderfully weird Witkiewicz.
al. Jerozolimskie 3. Tel: 022 621 1031. Open: Tue 10am–5pm, Wed & Thur 10am–4pm, Fri noon–9pm, Sat & Sun noon–6pm. Closed: Mon. Admission charge (except on Sat); extra fee for temporary exhibitions except on Sat.

Polish Army Museum

Positioned next door to the National Museum, the Polish Army Museum houses the largest collection of militaria in Poland, its oldest treasure being a gold helmet dating back to the time of the first Christian kings. The series of dimly lit rooms covers the chronological history of the Polish army, with display cases filled with the uniforms of winged hussars, regimental banners, medals, paintings of famous military moments and an assortment of weaponry. The final room has exhibits on World War II, with the uniforms and equipment of the Polish Home Army (Armia Krajowa) on display. The park outside is packed with tanks, aircraft and artillery pieces, and provides a fitting finale to your visit.
al. Jerozolimskie 3. Tel: 022 629 5271. Open: Thur–Sun 10am–4pm, Wed

10am–5pm. Closed: Mon & Tue. Last entry for groups only half an hour before closing. Admission charge except on Wed.

Railway Museum

A complete lack of English-language explanations means that many visitors will come away no more enlightened than when they entered, but this does little to prevent the Railway Museum being a highly recommended stop for anyone harbouring a passion for trains. Inside the museum is an overwhelming collection of engines, models and train sets, while the disused rail tracks outside are the resting place for a number of iron beasts, including steam engines, cable cars and an armoured train from World War II.
ul. Towarowa 1. Tel: 022 620 0480. Open: Mon 10am–2pm, Tue–Sun

10am–5pm. Admission charge except on Mon.

Zachęta Gallery

A must for fans of Polish art, this gallery possesses works by one of the founding members of Polish Art Nouveau – Stanisław Wyspiański – as well as Pankiewicz, the Gierymski brothers, Malczewski, and a number of paintings by Jan Matejko, including his historical epic *The Battle of Grunwald*. Considered one of the most important galleries in Poland, the Zachęta's primary function is to showcase modern art, and the regular exhibitions frequently draw some of the biggest names in the world.
pl. Małachowskiego 3 (entrance for visitors with disabilities at rear of premises). Tel: 022 827 5854. Open: Tue–Sun noon–8pm. Admission charge except on Thur.

The Arrival of the Legions in Warsaw, by Stanisław Bagińskie, at the Polish Army Museum

Museums and galleries

Gone but not forgotten

Flattened during World War II, Warsaw's rise from the rubble has proved little short of a building miracle, as well as a stirring tribute to the refusal of Varsovians to let their city die. But while the Old Town and New Town were painstakingly rebuilt, much of the remainder of the city was left to the mercy of communist architects, many inspired by the twin evils of concrete and prefabricated buildings.

A PLN200 million project is currently planned to rebuild the Saski Palace on pl. Piłsudskiego (see pp66–7). Although this slice of Warsaw history looks set to be brought back to life, spare a thought for the building that once took centre stage on pl. Piłsudskiego. Occupying what is now a granite-paved space was the Alexander Nevsky Orthodox Cathedral. Construction on this huge centre of worship lasted 18 years, and was finally completed just before the outbreak of World War I. Financed by taxes levied on the Polish people, the cathedral was to serve as a place of worship for the ruling Russian classes. When finished, it consisted of gold-plated onion domes, a 70m (230ft) tall tower and stunning interior arrangements. Alas, the collapse of

Imperial Russia meant that within a year of completion the cathedral had been commandeered by the German army. The moment Poland gained independence, discussions raged as to what to do with this symbol of Russian superiority. In the end it was decided to demolish the building with some 15,000 explosions carried out over a two-year period between 1924 and 1926. Fortunately, some of the treasures inside the cathedral were relocated to the Orthodox Church of St Mary Magdalene in Praga (see p119), one of only two Russian churches in Warsaw to survive this Polish desire for vengeance.

Close by, the corner of ul. Wierzbowa and ul. Fredry was once taken by the Brühl Palace, built at the whim of aristocrat Jerzy Ossoliński. Renovated at the tail end of the 17th century, it came into the possession of the government minister Heinrich von Brühl, a man largely credited with bringing Poland to its knees with his reckless financial policies and decision to dissolve parliament. Subsequent decades saw this palace – supposedly the most beautiful rococo building in Warsaw – become the domain of the wicked Grand Duke Constance, who installed dungeons in the basement.

In 1944 it was demolished by the Germans.

On to Krakowskie Przedmieście, and No 62 was once home to the Kazanowski Palace, designed by Tencella and completed in 1643. A century later Adam Kazanowski set about transforming it into one of Poland's most magnificent residences. Destroyed during the Swedish Deluge, it was rebuilt by the Lubomirski family who granted half the building to the Displaced Carmelites for use as a convent. Currently serving as the headquarters for the Polish charity Caritas, the courtyard still contains Renaissance buttresses, as well as a plaque that commemorates a scene in Henryk Sienkiewicz's novel *The Deluge*, which took place here: a fight between the hero Zagłoba and a team of monkeys.

The final word on vanished Warsaw must be directed towards the train station. Visitors to modern Warszawa Centralna will be forgiven for recoiling in horror. This wasn't always the case. Warsaw's first train station, Dworzec Wiedeński, was opened in 1845 based on a design by Enrico Marconi. Topped by a pair of 25m (82ft) towers, the building, found on al. Jerozolimskie, was demolished in the interwar years, its replacement facing an equally ignoble end at the hands of the retreating Nazis in 1944.

The Alexander Nevsky Orthodox Cathedral, which once filled pl. Piłsudskiego

Cemeteries

Warsaw's cemeteries date back to the 18th century and largely survived demolition during World War II. The best time to visit is when they are lit by thousands of flickering candles on the evening of All Saints' Day, 1 November, or on the anniversary of the Warsaw Uprising, 1 August. However, even outside religious holidays, the biggest cemeteries provide an impressive backdrop for a sombre stroll.

Powązki Cemetery

The oldest and most famous Catholic cemetery, Powązki features row upon row of the graves of well-known Poles, which are concentrated on the Avenue of Merit (al. Zasłużonych). The **St Karol Boromeusz Church** is located by the cemetery's main entrance, **St Honorata Gate**. Powązki's catacombs are the burial place of King Stanisław August Poniatowski's family. Other notable graves include that of Fryderyk Chopin's parents, which adjoins the grave of Stanisław Moniuszko, creator of the Polish National Opera. Polish politicians, scientists, writers and artists, as well as ordinary Poles, are buried in sculpted tombs, under beautifully designed statues and within intricately decorated chapels.
ul. Powązkowska 14.

Communal Cemetery

In the same district as Powązki, the Communal Cemetery is a military cemetery that was originally used for Russian soldiers, but was used throughout the last century for Polish soldiers and contains a symbolic cross for the 4,000-plus Polish prisoners murdered by Stalin's troops at Katyń at the beginning of World War II.
ul. Powązkowska 43/45.

Jewish Cemetery

The Jewish Cemetery contains graves and monuments of prominent Warsaw Jews. Ludwik Zamenhof, the optician who created the ill-fated Esperanto language in 1887, is buried here. A monument stands above the symbolic grave of Janusz Korczak, the doctor in charge of a Jewish orphanage who voluntarily went with his orphans to a Nazi death camp.
ul. Okopowa 49/51.

Protestant Reformed Cemetery and Augsburg Protestant Cemetery

Although smaller than the Catholic and Jewish cemeteries, the Protestant cemeteries have their own elaborate chapels and tombs. The mausoleum of the famous chocolate-making Wedel family is located in the Augsburg Cemetery.

Protestant Reformed Cemetery: ul.

Żytnia 42. Augsburg Protestant Cemetery: ul. Młynarska 54/56/58.

Muslim Tatar Cemetery

This cemetery was badly damaged during the World War II, one of the worst affected, but some of the graves have survived.

ul. Tatarska 8.

Russian Orthodox Cemetery

The Russian Orthodox Cemetery is not far from the Powązki cemetery. It holds the remains of Russians buried during the partition of Poland (1772–1918), and the later remains of Russian builders who died in accidents during the construction of the Palace of Culture and Science.

ul. Wolska 138/140.

Cemetery of the Warsaw Uprising

This cemetery is near the Russian Orthodox Cemetery, and contains the remains of 40,000 Varsovians that were exhumed from graves dotted around the city at the end of World War II.

ul. Wolska 174/176.

Bródno Cemetery

The largest cemetery in Poland is located across the river in Praga. It was established for the poor people of the neighbouring district, but now serves the entire city. Graves range from the simplest earth mounds with iron crosses to elaborately carved headstones.

ul. św. Wincentego 83.

Gravestones at the Jewish Cemetery

Pope John Paul II

Karol Józef Wojtyła was one of the most important figures in the history of Poland. When he died, thousands of Poles flocked to Vatican City in Rome to attend his funeral, and his picture is in every Catholic church in Poland. The Polish Pope is almost certain to be made a saint in the near future, bypassing the usual rules due to his particularly spectacular role and the mass adoration of the general public.

Karol Wojtyła was the second son of a tailor and a schoolteacher, born in 1920 in Wadowice, a town not far from Kraków. He and his father moved to Kraków when he was 18 so that the young Wojtyła could study literature and philosophy. When war broke out, he took a job in a quarry to avoid deportation and in 1942 began studying at an underground seminary. While Poles were being rounded up by the Nazis, Wojtyła was kept safe in the Archbishop of Kraków's residence and was ordained in 1946.

In 1962, as the Vatican was starting to debate the issues that would result in a reform of the Church, Wojtyła was made Bishop of Kraków. This was swiftly followed, five years later, by his becoming Cardinal. The Polish authorities, at this point, regarded him as a moderate individual, although he was in fact encouraging subversive activities such as ordaining underground priests in Czechoslovakia.

On 16 October 1978 Wojtyła became the first non-Italian Pope since Dutchman Adrian VI in 1523. He chose the name John Paul II (Jan Paweł in Polish) and visited Poland during his first year. The Mass he held in Warsaw was attended by hundreds of thousands of people. He famously boosted the Solidarity movement, contributing significantly to the breakdown of communism in his country.

Pope John Paul II held a mixture of surprisingly modern and strictly conservative beliefs. In 1985 the Vatican announced that homosexuality was an 'intrinsic moral evil' and in 1988 ruled out the ordination of women. The Pope himself also attracted criticism for his firm stance against the use of condoms, despite the deadly spread of AIDS around the world.

John Paul II responded promptly to world events throughout his life. When communism crumbled in Eastern Europe in 1989, he met Soviet

President Mikhail Gorbachev at the Vatican. During his lifelong struggle against communist influences, he also met Cuban President Fidel Castro and persuaded him to allow Cuban Christians to celebrate Christmas.

The Polish Pope did much to strengthen links with other religions. He travelled to Jerusalem and apologised for the role the Catholic Church played in the persecution of Jews. He became the first Pope to pray in a mosque and kiss the Koran. He also travelled to Greece and Armenia and reached out to Orthodox Christians. Differences remained, however, with Protestants, and particularly the Church of England, did not fare so well,

especially after the Church of England started to ordain women in the 1990s.

There are monuments to Pope John Paul II all over Warsaw, not to mention the main road named after him that goes right through the city. The Warsaw Uprising Museum (*see p15*) has a section dedicated to his influence in the country, including a recording of the Mass he held in 1978. The John Paul II Collection on pl. Bankowy is a collection of 450 paintings in a building that also hosts poetry and musical events. As well as the statue of the late Pope at the museum, there are others at the Field-Cathedral of the Polish Army and Holy Cross Church (*see pp56 & 95*).

Karol Wojtyła as a young priest in Poland

Wilanów Palace

It's not rare to hear of the park and palace complex of Wilanów being likened to Versailles, and such comparisons are by no means far-fetched, although Wilanów is on a somewhat smaller scale. A trip to Wilanów is a richly rewarding experience, offering a feast of Baroque opulence and a magnificent journey back to the time when Poland's empire stretched from the Black Sea to the Baltic Sea.

Wilanów Palace's history goes back to the 17th century when the Leszczyński family bought the area. They decided to build a palace, but their bold development project was left in ruins when Swedish troops ransacked the region. King John III Sobieski purchased the remains in 1676 and immediately ordered the construction of the palace to be resumed. What

The Baroque palace in Wilanów, summer residence of King John III Sobieski

resulted was an awe-inspiring Baroque masterpiece whose galleries and art treasures were first opened to the public in 1805. With much of its collection looted and its buildings damaged during World War II, Wilanów was in a state of abject disrepair when it passed into the hands of the post-war government (or rather, was seized by it). A meticulous programme of restoration was embarked upon, and by 1962 the palace was again open to visitors.

The exquisite decoration of recently renovated Wilanów Palace

Today its corridors and chambers offer an extraordinary glimpse into the world of the Polish aristocracy, with English-language audio guides available for those who wish to truly immerse themselves in the historical experience. Works by Flemish and Italian painters, suits of armour and elaborate frescoes adorn the interiors, with a separate room dedicated to priceless Etruscan ceramics. Visitors are also given the opportunity to tour the living quarters of the former regents based here, with the highlight being King Sobieski's room – his bed is covered by a canopy of Turkish fabrics taken as the spoils of war following his victory over the Ottoman Empire at the gates of Vienna in 1683.

Those looking to escape the school groups that scramble noisily around the interiors can do so by visiting the palace's gardens. These were regularly remodelled and the result is a rich tapestry of styles: wander around English rose gardens, a Chinese arbour and a two-level classic Baroque garden.

Along the way visual distractions include a human-made island accessed by a Roman-style bridge, a neo-Gothic mausoleum and a statue commemorating the Battle of Raszyn in 1809. To make the most of these spectacular gardens, visit in summer when classical music concerts are held in the grounds and boats paddle visitors around the lakes.

On your way out of the palace complex, pop into the **Wilanów Poster Museum**. Occupying the palace's former stables, this was the first poster museum in the world when it was unveiled in 1968 and still remains the largest. Two halls house more than 55,000 items, including works by Andy Warhol and some 35,000 Polish posters dating from 1892 to 2002. If you like what you see, you might be able to take it home with you: many pieces that make up the collection have been reproduced in souvenir postcard format.
Bus No 180 runs to Wilanów *(see pp64–5).*

Modern architecture

As Warsaw was levelled by the Nazis, post-war city planners were able to rebuild the city from scratch. A quick look out of virtually any window in town shows how bad a job they made of it. Surviving bullet-battered Art Nouveau and rebuilt Renaissance styles rub shoulders with grim socialist realism and a heavy dose of 1960s monstrosities. Luckily, however, the collapse of the Iron Curtain heralded a new dawn for the city: a surge of investment and a gold rush for riches.

The raw capitalism that has since gripped the city has transformed it into a seething metropolis. Warsaw's defining icon – the Palace of Culture and Science (*see pp30–31*) – is fast disappearing amid a forest of sparkling skyscrapers. Two such buildings are hotels, the Marriott and the InterContinental. While the Marriott may appear a faceless glass block, its interiors play host to a wealth of riches, topped with a panoramic 40th-floor bar that gives sweeping views of the Warsaw skyline. French-born 'Spider Man' Alain Robert chose a novel way of getting to this bar, scaling the structure with his bare hands before being refused entry for not meeting the dress code. The neighbouring InterContinental – a daring construction balanced on three legs – features similar luxuries.

The area around the Palace of Culture and Science has undergone aggressive redesign, with the most remarkable development being Złote Tarasy, unveiled in 2007. This hyper-modern mall has a show-stealing 10,000sq m (107,600sq ft) glass roof (thankfully, it's domed and flows downwards to prevent snow from building up). An even bolder structure

The Metropolitan Building by Lord Foster

The award-winning Warsaw University Library building

is planned for Złota 44 – Daniel Libeskind's first Polish project. This 192m (630ft) residential tower, assuming that it is ever finished, will feature state-of-the-art penthouses and a daring design reminiscent of a ship's sail. He is not the only eminent architect who has been attracted to Warsaw. In 2003 Sir Norman Foster's Metropolitan Building was completed in pl. Piłsudskiego. Built at a cost of US$110 million, the structure scooped the prize for Best Business Centre in the 2004 MIPIM awards. The 'love it or hate it' design is pentagon shaped, with granite fins jutting from its seven floors, and features a courtyard fountain and luxury shops. Directly opposite once stood the Saski Palace (*see pp66–7*). The plan is that a careful replica of the grand palace that was dynamited by the Nazis will, within the next few years, grace Warsaw once again. Such projects are symbolic of the desire to renovate and rebuild buildings that were either flattened or left to crumble after World War II, with the Art Deco Rialto Hotel (*ul. Wilcza 73*) and the top-end retail/dining/office Dom Dochodowy complex (*pl. Trzech Krzyży 3*) being supreme examples of this. Less than a decade ago both buildings were little more than blackened ruins; now they serve as haunts of the stars.

Although many of Warsaw's most inspiring structures are off-limits to all but corporate types and hotel guests, the **Warsaw University Library** is open to the public (*ul. Dobra 56/66*). Opened in 2002, the principal claim to fame here is the rooftop garden, complete with bridges, pathways and hillocks. Aside from dazzling views, the gardens capture Warsaw's new look: fresh, bold and innovative.

Getting away from it all

There are a number of towns, cities and villages reasonably close to Warsaw that make good destinations for full- or half-day trips. Public transport outside the city is somewhat challenging, but you should be able to get to these spots without too much trouble.

Kampinos

The Kampinos National Park is 40km (25 miles) northwest of the centre of Warsaw, making it the most accessible national park in Poland, as well as one of only two nature reserves in the world to lie partly within a capital city. Established in 1959, in 2000 it was classified by UNESCO as a World Biosphere Reserve, and makes for an easy trip from Warsaw. The second-largest national park in Europe, the forest is home to a rich variety of flora and fauna, including 69 protected species of flower, 83 endangered species of animal and a 400-year-old oak. Projects to reintroduce beaver, elk (the park's symbol) and lynx have proved largely successful over the years, and the park now contains a staggering range of wildlife: white-tailed eagles, black storks, 14 species of bat and 6 of reptile. It also has 31 species of mosquito, all of which consider you a walking meal. Although this was once the hunting ground of choice for Polish monarchs, today its inhabitants find themselves strictly protected under Polish law. The area is criss-crossed with hiking, cycling and horse-riding trails, and so offers a host of sightseeing opportunities. These include the classical manor house in Tułowice

A young moose in Kampinos National Park

The Duke of Mazovia's castle in Czersk, once the capital of the region

Kampinos that was used as the rebel headquarters during the ill-fated 1863 January Uprising. During World War II Kampinos was used as a training ground and base camp for many of the insurgents who participated in the Warsaw Uprising, and the cemetery near Palmiry village holds the remains of 2,115 members of the Polish intelligentsia who were executed by the Nazis.

Czersk

About 40 kilometres (25 miles) up the Vistula River from Warsaw is a small town called Czersk. Once it was the capital of Mazovia, but now it's just another place where people come from, not a place people go to.

Despite its rather impressive castle, built in 1388, Czersk steadily lost importance over time as Warsaw became the dominant city in the region and then the country, especially after the Vistula River moved to the other side of the flood plain and left the castle 4km (2½ miles) away. King Zygmunt's second wife, Bona Sforza, was very taken with the place – she ordered the towers to be raised to their present height of 30m (98ft) and the orchards to be planted around the castle. Next to take an interest was George II Rákóczi, prince of Transylvania. In 1667 his troops destroyed most of the castle and the town for good measure. Grand Marshal Franciszek Bieliński (the marshal after

The birthplace of Fryderyk Chopin, now a museum

whom ul. Marszałkowska is named) was a supporter of Czersk and ordered some rebuilding work to be carried out from 1762 to 1766. These days the town is a provincial backwater and just has the ruin of the castle, the orchards and an excellent view of the Vistula plain. Fortunately, two of the three towers are accessible and offer spectacular views of the area. You can even rent the castle for your own events.

Żelazowa Wola

Żelazowa Wola is about 50km (31 miles) from central Warsaw and stands on the banks of the Utrata River. It is best known as the birthplace of Fryderyk Chopin and now is the home of a museum to the great composer. While the manor house that contains the museum is strictly speaking where Chopin was born, it's debatable how much he would recognise today. In his time it was just the annexe of a much larger house; much of the present structure was built in the 1920s and virtually none of the furniture is original. The seven rooms are fairly interesting, but if you've arrived at the same time as a tour bus, you'll see precious little: the place is tiny and will be packed.

A better option is to wander around the park. Covering some 7ha (17 acres), it was planted with different types of trees and bushes from all over Poland. It also has various foreign trees, including American pines, Californian firs and Japanese barberries, but the native willows on the banks of the river are the most attractive. You're more likely to feel the spirit of Chopin sitting under the willow trees watching the river roll by than by looking at furniture that might resemble what was there when he was a boy. There are also piano concerts held at 11am and 3pm every Sunday (*May–Sept*).

Minibuses to Żelazowa Wola run in summer from the Fryderyk Chopin Museum at Ostrogskich palace, ul. Okólnik 1 in central Warsaw. Tel: 022 827 5473 ext. 108 for times and tickets.

Konstancin-Jeziorna

Konstancin-Jeziorna is a very pleasant little spa town located 20km (12½ miles) from central Warsaw and is easily reached by bus. The town escaped significant damage in World War II and so, as you'd expect from what has been a resort town for more than 100 years, it has a good number of attractive villas, many in the Art Nouveau style that was popular in the early 20th century.

Several old parks are ideal for taking a stroll and enjoying good clean air. If this isn't healthy enough for you, head for the Park Zdrojowy (Health Park). It has an open-air 'inhalitorium': benches surrounded by walls made of blackthorn branches with saltwater flowing down them. As the water evaporates, a special microclimate is produced; it's very much like going to the seafront and having a breath of sea air. Locals say the air is very beneficial to your health and few people would deny that it's an ideal spot for a refreshing snooze after lunch.

Bus: The best choice is No 700 from outside Warsaw Central Station (Warszawa Centralny); it takes 50–60 minutes to reach Konstancin-Jeziorna but the last bus back to the city centre is usually not much later than 6pm.

One of the many beautiful old villas in Konstancin-Jeziorna

Łódź

Łódź is easily accessible from Warsaw; trains leave the Central Station regularly and the journey takes about two hours. With a population that touches 800,000, Łódź ranks as Poland's second city, as well as one of its youngest. A direct product of the Industrial Revolution, Łódź was little more than a quiet rural community at the start of the 19th century. That changed with the dawn of the Industrial Revolution: the city became a key centre of production, manufacturing textiles destined for the markets of Imperial Russia. The factories and blackened tenements that once housed the proletariat survive to this day, covering vast swathes of central Łódź and lending the city a gritty urban edge that has seen it called 'the Manchester of Poland'.

Overseeing this transformation from backwater town to simmering metropolis was Izrael Poznański, a man whose huge factory mills gave employment to thousands. His vast palace (*ul. Ogrodowa 15*) has since been turned into the city museum, a superb romp through the city's history. Close by is the site of his former factory, nowadays the Manufaktura leisure and shopping complex: a never-ending riot of 19th-century red-brick structures. Many retail opportunities are presented inside, though the real highlights are the after-work venues that include a microbrewery, industrial museum, nightclubs, kids' centre and the most high-class dining room in town, L'ecru. A Jew by birth, Poznański was buried in the Jewish Cemetery inside a spectacular mausoleum that brings to mind 1960s horror flicks.

The Jewish influence on Łódź is impossible to ignore. The aforementioned cemetery is reputed to be the largest in Europe, with more than 180,000 graves, including the mass graves of 45,000 Jews killed during the Holocaust. Before World War II the Jewish population of the city was almost a quarter of a million. Once the city was incorporated into the Third Reich, it found itself home to one of the most notorious ghettoes of the war. To the north of the city Radegast train

Łódź Cathedral by night

The White Factory, a monument to Łódź's industrial history

station, where more than 200,000 Jews and gypsies were herded into cattle trucks bound for the gas chambers, has been faithfully preserved as a sombre tribute to the Holocaust.

All trips to Łódź centre on one street: measuring over 4km (2½ miles), ul. Piotrkowska is Europe's longest pedestrian highway, with a battalion of rickshaw drivers on hand to help your journey along it. The rickshaws also prove a great way to admire the peeling Art Nouveau façades that line the street, as well as providing ample opportunity to pick out the best bars and beer gardens for which Łódź has become known – for recommendations check out the English-language guide *In Your Pocket Łódź*. However, the real beauty of ul. Piotrkowska lies in the detail. Take, for example, the Hollywood-style 'Walk of Fame' starting outside the Grand Hotel – a direct homage to the stars of the Polish screen, many of whom, such as Roman Polański, cut their teeth at the local film academy. Don't miss a visit to the Museum of Cinematography (*pl. Zwycięstwa 1*) to learn more.

Trains leave for Łódź from Warsaw Central Station regularly and the journey takes about 2 hours.

Shopping

The options for shopping in Warsaw have changed radically in recent years. In the early 1990s huge outdoor markets were the best and often only choice for shoppers. Now the city has two of the five largest malls in central and eastern Europe. It's still not a place for shopaholics but it does offer a good range of options.

The three main shopping centres in the city are **Arkadia** (*al. Jana Pawła II 82*), **Złote Tarasy** (*in the heart of the city, next to Warsaw Central Station*) and **Galeria Mokotów** (*ul. Wołoska 12, about 25 minutes by tram from the centre*). **Galeria Centrum** (*ul. Marszałkowska 104/122*) is smaller but worth investigating. All offer a good selection of shops. The clothing stores

are mainly the same chains as found in other parts of Europe and prices are also much the same. Warsaw has a good number of antique shops that often have some attractive items. But if you want to export anything produced before 1945 (including books), you will need a special permit. Obtaining one takes time (at least two weeks), provides an introduction to Polish

Hand-painted Bolesławiec pottery makes a perfect souvenir

BOLESŁAWIEC POTTERY

Pottery from the Bolesławiec factory is very popular and prices here are sometimes a quarter of those charged in Western Europe. The hand-painted pieces are all marked on the base with the name of the person who made them. The Cepelia shops have a reasonable range and also stock folk art and similar products. By far the best place for choice and value is the Bolesławiec factory shop (*ul. Prosta, close to Rondo ONZ*).

bureaucracy, which is among the worst in the world, and costs money. But if you simply cannot live without a particular antique, or if you're a serious masochist, contact the Assessment and Evaluation Department of the **National Museum** (*ul. Smolna 14, Warsaw. Tel: 022 828 0208. Open: Tue–Fri 10am–1pm. No English spoken*).

What to buy

The most obvious gift is amber jewellery. Poland has one of the largest amber industries in the world and prices can be excellent. There are a number of shops in the Old Town with prices set especially for tourists, and jewellers in the main shopping centres and the Nowy Świat area often offer better value. Street traders are best avoided unless you want amber-coloured plastic instead of real amber.

Another recommended Polish speciality is linen; it's very high quality and reasonably priced. The three shops on ul. Senatorska are probably the best places to try: all have a good selection, offer hand-embroidered options and accept orders for custom-made products (ask nicely, and for a fee they will even post the finished product to you). There are also a couple of reasonable shops on ul. Marszałkowska and a few places in the Old Town (with prices that reflect the high rents charged in that area). Handmade Polish lace is virtually guaranteed to put a smile on the face of anybody's grandmother. Good places to buy include **Cepelia** shops (there are four in town, the most central is at the corner of al. Jerozolimskie and ul. Marszałkowska) and some souvenir shops in the Old Town.

Some of the best lace is made in the village of Koniaków: as well as making Vatican altar-cloths, the village has recently branched out with a line of handmade lace thongs (probably not recommended for your grandmother). Another name to look for is Bobowa.

Złote Tarasy, Warsaw's latest shopping destination of choice

Entertainment

Warsaw has long been the cultural capital of Poland and that status is reflected in the number of concerts, plays, operas, exhibitions and other events on offer. The city's nightlife gets better and better every year: the number of bars has grown hugely, their quality much improved, and its clubs are some of the best anywhere in central Europe.

What's on

The best source of information is Poland's leading English-language news publication: the *New Poland Express*. This free newspaper has a good coverage of the cultural events in Warsaw and beyond. The electronic version is available via email and has a listing of each week's events (*www.npe.pl*). The *Warsaw Voice* comes out weekly and has detailed information written in a memorably unique style. *Aktivist* magazine has an exhaustive list of events aimed at the younger crowd, but is in Polish and has an appalling layout and attitude. Warsaw's gay community has its own publication, *A.Y.O.R. (At Your Own Risk)*; available free at most gay-friendly venues, it lists each month's events.

Catch a show

Warsaw is home to more than 40 theatres, including many of Poland's best. Prime among these is the **National Theatre** in the building of the same name on pl. Teatralny (*see pp60–61*). Unfortunately for tourists, the vast majority of performances at all theatres are in Polish, which makes keeping up with the plot something of a challenge. A notable exception is the **Jewish Theatre** (*pl. Grzybowski 12/16*); it has performances only in Yiddish

GETTING TICKETS

Most venues have a box office that sells tickets, but opening hours can vary wildly and you're unlikely to find anybody who speaks English. **EMPIK** stores (*locations include ul. Nowy Świat 15/17, ul. Marszałkowska 106/122 and the three main shopping malls: Złote Tarasy, Arkadia and Galeria Mokotów*) are better; they sell tickets to all the big events and can usually find an English-speaking staff member if you need to talk about seat choices. Another option for big events is *www.ticketpro.pl*, which has an English-language version and offers 'electronic tickets'. If you're after theatre tickets, **Kasy Teatralne i Estradowe Kasy Teatralne ZASP** (*al. Jerozolimskie 25. Tel: 022 621 9454*) is a good place to try.

(some also have an English translation via headphones).

The **Roma Musical Theatre** (*ul. Nowogrodzka 49. Tel: 022 628 7071*) stages musicals and light opera. In recent years it has won critical acclaim for its productions of *Cats*, *Miss Saigon* and *Dance of the Vampires* (based on Roman Polański's screenplay of the film *The Fearless Vampire Killers* from 1967). Ticket prices range from PLN35 to PLN85 and almost all productions are in Polish.

Other music- and song-based shows in languages you probably won't understand are found at the **National Opera** (the same building as the National Theatre). The company performs works by both Polish and foreign composers and regularly features major figures of the international scene. Also in the same building is the **Warsaw Ballet Company**. The standard of both is generally very high, but a summer break is taken each year, so don't plan any

The Roma Musical Theatre stages well-known musicals and opera

FOTOPLASTYKON

The word *fotoplastykon* literally means 'peep show' but this place certainly will never be mistaken for a porn show. It dates back more than 100 years, a piece of the Warsaw from the turn of the 20th century, and is unfairly ignored by visitors and Varsovians alike. The Fotoplastykon (better translated as 'stereogram') has seating for 24 people and shows 3D photographs. Shows change regularly and make use of the owner's collection of 3,600 stereographic pictures; the most popular is of Warsaw from 1895 to 1965. Once these devices were entertainment for the masses but now they are almost extinct – catch a stereographic show while you can.

al. Jerozolimskie 51. Open: Tue & Thur 3–7pm, Sat 11am–3pm. Admission charge.

trips to the opera or the ballet if you're here in July, August or September.

Also essential for highbrow culture vultures (and highly recommended for anybody with any interest in music) is the **Orkiestra Filharmonii Narodowej w Warszawie** (Warsaw National Philharmonic Orchestra). Founded in 1901, this orchestra is one of the oldest and finest in Europe; during the interwar years it was a who's who of Polish classical musicians, and its conductors included Strauss, Stravinsky and Ravel. After losing its home and half its members during World War II, both the orchestra and its home (*ul. Jasna 5*) are now back to their best. The National Philharmonic has been the host of the Chopin International Piano Competition since its inception in 1927. The competition is held every five years, the next being in October 2015.

If choral music is your cup of tea, enjoy the regular concerts (and superb acoustics) at the **Evangelical Reformed Church** (*al. Solidarności 74*). Particularly recommended are performances by the Nowa Orkiestra Kameralna.

Casinos

Warsaw is never going to match Las Vegas, but there are a few options if you fancy a flutter, almost all at the major hotels. All have strict dress code (jacket and shirt), and you won't get in if you don't have your passport. Good bets (excuse the pun) include: the **Hotel Victoria**, if Texas Hold 'em is your game; the **Warsaw Hilton**, probably the best casino and certainly the most modern; and the **Marriott**, one of

The Evangelical Reformed Church

the largest casinos in town and home to some particularly tasteful stained glass.

Clubbing and music

As with most cities, the club scene in Warsaw changes fast. **Piekarnia** (*ul. Młocińska 11*) has been arguably the best club in the city for nearly a decade and still has big-name DJs, although it's slightly past its best. **Klubo Kawiarnia** (*ul. Czackiego 3/5*) is a little hard to find but worth the effort most nights of the week; it is regularly packed at 4am on a Thursday. **Luzztro** (*al. Jerozolimskie 6*) opens on Friday afternoon and closes on Tuesday morning, by which time it's mainly full of people who illustrate exactly why taking drugs is a bad idea. **Platinium** (*ul. Fredy 6*) offers superb design and expensive drinks, but the door policy involves both the highest fashion and trophy girlfriends.

If you're looking for live music, the **Hard Rock Café** (*Złote Tarasy, ul. Zlota 59*) is home to regular live performances and is almost exactly the same as every other Hard Rock Café on the planet. Alternatively, try the **Warsaw Tortilla Factory** (*corner of ul. Wilcza and ul. Poznańska*); it has bands or soloists at least a couple of times a week and legendary cocktails that produce hangovers of an epic scale.

Tygmont (*ul. Mazowiecka 6/8*) is unquestionably the best place for jazz in Warsaw, but talking while the artists play is discouraged, often by the artists themselves.

Lesbian, Gay, Bisexual, Transgender (LGBT) Warsaw

Homosexuality is legal in Poland and there is no difference in the age of consent from that of heterosexuals. However, many politicians openly condemn homosexuals because such views win votes. In 2005 Kazimierz Marcinkiewicz, then prime minister, said, 'If a person tries to infect others with their homosexuality, then the state must intervene.' While the late president of Poland, Lech Kaczyński, was mayor of Warsaw he twice banned the annual Gay Pride march, reportedly saying, 'I am not willing to meet perverts' when the organising group suggested a meeting. More worrying is a 2006 statement by Krzysztof Bosak, an MP from the then governing coalition: 'Violence is bad but there is no way you can protest against this abnormality [homosexuality] without violence.'

Warsaw has a small but lively Lesbian, Gay, Bisexual, Transgender (LGBT) scene. **Utopia** (*ul. Jasna 1*) is the best-known gay club but widely referred to as the 'cretins' choice' by critics and

The Olympic Casino at the Warsaw Hilton

ADULT WARSAW

There are a number of lap-dancing clubs in town. **SoGo** (*ul. Smolna 15*) is the biggest, but few of the 50 dancers can actually dance. **Playhouse Gentlemen's Club** (*al. Solidarności 82a*) is a subterranean affair allegedly featuring 57 ladies. **Las Vegas** is reputedly the best and the most expensive; not that the other places need any lessons in how to extract cash from punters. All these clubs seem more tolerant than venues in Western Europe, but there are very strictly enforced rules: breaking those may well result in a trip to hospital. It is illegal to pay for sex in Poland, so why there are (according to official estimates) more than 1,500 brothels is anybody's guess. Flyers for escort agencies are found on car windscreens and clog gutters all over the city. The adverts are everywhere, but tales of sexually transmitted diseases (STDs) are almost as common.

allegedly unwilling to admit lesbians. A far better place is **Tomba Tomba** (*ul. Brzozowa 37*), a straight-friendly gay club and one of the best clubs of any type in Poland. Also well worth checking out is **Rasko** (*ul. Burakowska 12*); the entertainment can be anything from drag queen shows to karaoke and the crowd is friendly. The best gay bar is **Lodi Dodi** (*ul. Wilcza 23*), a tiny bar on the ground floor and three rooms in the basement. **Bastylia** (*ul. Mokotowska 17, on the corner with pl. Zbawiciela*) is the most popular choice with the lesbian community, although the LGBT crowd is only there during evenings and weekends, and serves superb crêpes. It also has wonderful staff and very pleasant customers.

Children

Warsaw has a reasonable amount to offer younger visitors, but both standards and range of choice can be slightly below the levels that residents of Western Europe may be used to.

Blue City

A bad-weather option is Blue City shopping centre. Blue City is no ordinary shopping centre (although it has a good selection of shops): spread over six levels, it has more space than it needs. Starting at the bottom, it has a go-kart track on level −2. A skate-park (called Kamuflage) on level −1 is for all skate fans from beginners to professionals and there is a good selection of ramps and quarter-pipes. On level 4 is Magic City, which features a video arcade and an area called Inca Play for younger children. Other spaces in Blue City are taken up by the Event Club, which runs regular indoor paintball and laser-tag games.
al. Jerozolimskie 179.

Outdoors

The playground in Ujazdowski Park is one of the best in Warsaw and within walking distance of Ujazdowski Castle. Older children should have plenty of fun on the monkey bars and the giant spider web, but under-fives might find the sandbox and swings boring and the other equipment too difficult. Another good choice is Park Dreszera, which has slides and monkey bars, and the spider webs are built for all ages.
Ujazdowski Park: corner of ul. Piękna & al. Ujazdowskie. Park Dreszera: corner of al. Niepodległości & Odyńca.

University Library

University libraries are not high on the list of places to take children, but Warsaw's new University Library building is very much an exception. The main attraction is the garden that covers the entire roof, more than 2,000sq m (21,520sq ft). This is linked to a lower garden, which covers 15,000sq m (161,400sq ft) around the northern end of the building, by stairs running alongside waterfalls.

The basement of the building is home to the Hula Kula family entertainment centre. There are two

indoor playgrounds: one for children younger than seven (called Hula Land) and the other for those aged seven to thirteen (Hula Park), as well as special bowling lanes for children. There is also a climbing wall, the biggest and reputedly the best in Warsaw, which can be used by all children except the very youngest. *Dobra 56/66. University Library Garden. Open: May–Sept 9am–8pm, Apr & Oct 9am–6pm, Nov–Mar (no access to roof area) 9am–3pm. Free admission.*
Hula Land. Open: Mon–Fri noon–8pm, Sat & Sun 10am–8pm.
Hula Park. Open: Mon–Fri 4–8pm, Sat & Sun 10am–8pm.

Climbing wall. Open: Mon–Fri 4.30–9.30pm, Sat & Sun 11.30am–6pm.

Warsaw Zoo

Warsaw Zoo has some 5,000 animals from more than 300 species. There is an area called the Fairyland Zoo especially for children, where they can look at and feed the sheep, pigs, rabbits and other domestic animals. Conditions for the animals have improved but there is still a long way to go. Keep an eye out for the two zebras named Unnur and Ubi; their godmother is Miss World 2005. *ul. Ratuszowa 1/3. Tel: 022 619 4041. www.zoo.waw.pl. Open: 9am–7pm. Closes earlier during winter. Admission charge.*

Children

The Fairyland Zoo at Warsaw Zoo, a favourite with younger Varsovians

Sweet Warsaw

If you ask a Varsovian to name a maker of something sweet, it's a safe bet you'll hear one of two names in reply: Wedel or Blikle. No matter how strict your calorie counting, you shouldn't leave Warsaw without trying at least one of the masters of diet-busting.

The Wedel brand dates back to 1851 when a young German confectioner named Karol Wedel came to Warsaw and opened a small workshop on ul. Miodowa. His son, Emil Wedel, took over the business and moved it to a lavish fin-de-siècle-style house on ul. Szpitalna in 1894. Emil's Pijalnia Czekolady (Chocolate Parlour) shop and café is still in the same beautiful house on ul. Szpitalna today (see p105). The firm isn't back to its glory days – between the wars, it had shops as far away as London and Paris – but it survived the communist era (although it was taken from the Wedel family and renamed '22 Lipca' to celebrate the founding of the Polish communist state in Lublin on 22 July 1944). After a close brush with destruction in the 1990s, the company set out on an ambitious expansion programme: it now has cafés in all Warsaw's main shopping centres. Better still, the original Wedel Chocolate Parlour on ul. Szpitalna was recently renovated and brought back to its very best. But be warned before you try it: Wedel hot chocolate is arguably the most addictive substance known to humankind.

Another company that has been satisfying Varsovian sugar cravings for nearly a century and a half is Blikle. The business was set up in 1869 when Antoni Blikle opened a Viennese-style café at Nowy Świat 33 with a confectioner's shop next door at No 35. The firm's products, in particular its signature doughnut, rapidly became huge hits with Varsovians and visitors alike; Charles de Gaulle was a regular during his years in Warsaw. Although the firm's premises were destroyed in World War II, there was never any serious question about it returning to the same two shops in the rebuilt Nowy Świat. However, were it not for the pugnaciously determined character of Jerzy Blikle (Antoni's grandson), it's likely that A Blikle would have met the same fate as E Wedel: seized by the state and lost to the family forever. Jerzy simply would not surrender his shop. He was forbidden to employ more than 40 people (which still made Blikle one of the largest private companies in the country) and suffered from various degrees of harassment, even being arrested several times for crimes that included buying 15 eggs from a retailer instead of a wholesaler. But his willingness to roll dough with his employees (and the fact that most communist ministers wanted Blikle products at their state receptions) kept the firm alive until communism died. In 1990 the fourth Blikle generation took over when Andrzej Blikle gave up being a professor of mathematics in order to run his father's firm. Under his leadership the company has expanded and now has 240 employees, 8 of its own cafés and 9 franchised cafés, all serviced by the firm's one and only bakery.

The Wedel shop on ul. Szpitalna, a mecca for those with a sweet tooth

Sport and leisure

Although Warsaw is far from being a sporting mecca, most of the usual suspects are available if you feel the need to do some sport or to simply watch other people doing it.

There's an outdoor ice rink in front of the Palace of Culture and Science in winter (usually from the beginning of December) but only if the temperature is below 10°C (50°F). If you're willing to pay PLN8/6 for half an hour, head for the rink at **Torwar II** (*ul. Łazienkowska 6a. Tel: 022 625 5306. Open: Thur, Sat & Sun*). There are a couple of places that offer bowling, pool tables and so on; **Galeria Mokotów** (*ul. Wołoska 12*) is one, with 150,000sq m (1,614,000sq ft) of shops too. Another choice is **Hula Kula** (*ul. Dobra 56/66, see pp152–3*). Warsaw Golf and Country Club is the only golf course and it's in Rajszew, 25km (15½ miles) north of Warsaw (*green fees are PLN125 Mon, PLN225 Tue–Fri, PLN375 Sat & Sun*). If you're after a little more adrenalin, try karting at **Imola** (*ul. Puławska 33. www.imola.pl*). If you're after a lot more adrenalin, speak to the people at the **Adrenalin Factory** (*ul. Modlińska 342. Tel: 022 819 0206. www.fabrykaadrenaliny.pl*). They organise everything from paintballing to quad-bike riding to zorbing to tank driving.

Watching sport

Warsaw has two top-flight football teams: Legia and Polonia. In 2011 Legia move into a new 100 million złoty stadium. The fixture list and ticket info are at *www.legia.com*. Polonia matches are not recommended: being a Polonia

EURO 2012

Poland will be hosting the 2012 European football championships jointly with Ukraine. The news was greeted with much joy, partly because host nation status will save the Polish team from their usual failure to qualify and partly because it requires the government to finally invest in some infrastructure. As host city of the opening game, two other group games, a quarter-final and a semi-final, Warsaw is being treated to a new national stadium, a second metro line, a second airport and modernisation of the tram and train networks. Some of those projects may even be finished in time for the tournament. Possibly.

fan is a truly soul-crushing infliction. Hooliganism is still an occasional problem for the Polish game, so pay the extra few złoty for seats in the main stand. Cheering for the away team will lead to problems.

Fancy losing your money on a donkey that sits down in the middle of the race for a rest, and only narrowly avoids winning the race because of a sudden burst of pace over the final furlong? Służewiec race track is the place. Details can be found at the Polish Jockey Club website, *www.pkwk.pl*

If there's a British (or Irish) sporting event you simply cannot miss, head to either **Warsaw Tortilla Factory** (*ul. Wilcza 46. Tel: 022 621 8622*) or **Jimmy Bradley's** (*ul. Sienna 39. Tel: 022 654 6656*). Both have vast satellite dishes that receive every channel broadcast in Britain and they show all the big games, weekend and mid-week. Bradley's also shows NFL games on Sundays.

Warsaw's new national stadium is under construction

Food and drink

Polish food usually displays its roots as good honest fuel for people doing a good honest day's work in the fields. Gastronomes hate it but food lovers adore it: it's not pretentious and it certainly is tasty. If you were on a diet when you arrived in Warsaw, you're pretty much guaranteed not to be when you leave.

There are three main ingredients: meat (almost always pork), potato and cabbage. Any good meal features all three. Vegetarians have problems in Poland; the idea of using no meat-based products while cooking is anathema to most chefs. Lard is so popular here that it is even served by itself to spread on bread (*smalec* is the name, and it goes amazingly well with beer). Fish, apart from pickled herring, is usually viewed with suspicion, and in a restaurant any fish other than trout or salmon is likely to have been frozen.

Specialities

One of the essential Polish specialities is *pierogi*. These are often mistranslated as 'dumplings' but are actually similar to ravioli. They first appeared on Polish tables shortly after King Zygmunt I married an Italian woman, Bona Sforza, who brought to Poland both Italian cooks and a fashion for Italian food. *Pierogi* are semicircular pockets of unleavened dough and are filled with almost anything edible. More common versions include *pierogi ruskie* (filled with potatoes and cheese), *pierogi z kapustą i grzybami* (with cabbage and mushroom) and *pierogi z kapustą i mięsem* (with cabbage and minced meat). They are also served as dessert: *pierogi z serem* (with sweet cheese), *pierogi z jagodami* (with berries) and *pierogi z truskawkami* (with strawberries). Good places to try *pierogi*

Pierogi ruskie

include **Pierogarnia na Bednarskiej** (*ul. Bednarska 28/30. Tel: 022 828 0392*), **Zapiecek** (*al. Jerozolimskie 28. Tel: 022 826 7484*), **Pierogarnia przy Mokotowskiej** (*ul. Mokotowska 12. Tel: 022 625 5371*) and **Pierrogeria** (*pl. Konstytucji 2. Tel: 022 654 4444*).

A good starter to try is *śledź* (marinated pickled herring). This is usually served with onion and comes in two versions: *śledź w oleju* (with oil) and *śledź w śmietanie* (with sour cream). Soups are very popular in Poland. One of the best is *żurek*, made from fermented rye and served with slices of sausage, pieces of ham and a hardboiled egg. Beetroot soup is so popular there are many versions, including: *barszcz czysty z uszkami* (clear soup with mushroom-filled ravioli), *barszcz ukraiński* (with cream) and *chłodnik* (with sour milk and young beet leaves, served cold). Other Polish specials include *flaki* (tripe with marjoram) and *czernina*, which is made from chicken broth and duck's blood.

A highly recommended main course is *bigos*. Usually translated as 'hunter's stew', it is virtually the national dish. Almost every family has its own recipe but ingredients always include cabbage (often both fresh and fermented), various types of meat and sausage, tomato and assorted herbs. Three other specialities are *gołąbki* (meat and rice wrapped in cabbage leaves), *kotlet schabowy* (pork chop hammered thin, coated in breadcrumbs, fried and served with potatoes and cabbage) and *golonka* (pig's trotters roasted in their skin, often with a bit of hair still attached).

With the exception of *naleśniki* (thin pancakes, usually served *z serem*, with sweet cheese, but sometimes with cooked fruit), Poles tend to prefer cakes to other desserts. *Makowiec* is a particularly good choice: a rolled cake filled with poppy seeds. *Szarlotka* is usually called 'apple pie' but is often more of a tart than a pie. *Sernik* is cheesecake but a type that is baked. *Pączki* are jam-filled doughnuts, and *piernik* is gingerbread, often filled with jam or fruit.

Żurek soup served in a loaf of bread

Restaurants and cafés

Warsaw has restaurants serving food from all corners of the earth, with more springing up every month, so even the fussiest gourmets should find something to suit them. Standards range from ultra-high-end (although nowhere in the city yet has a Michelin star) to the most basic of canteens.

Recently, the lines between restaurant and bar have become blurred. Many bars, including all but one of those listed on *pp163–5*, now serve food and some can be very good. Service is getting better and usually worth tipping. However, some places have a 10 per cent service charge (usually hidden in the menu in tiny print), so check the bill before you tip. Avoid saying 'thank you' (*dziękuje*) when you pay a bill – it means 'keep the change'.

The price guide is for two people having a starter and a main course each but with no drinks (wine tends to be expensive, with prices usually starting around PLN100 per bottle; beer is about PLN10 per 500ml). Most restaurants are open from about noon and stop taking orders for food at around 9pm.

★　　PLN50 or less
★★　PLN51–PLN100
★★★　PLN101–PLN150
★★★★　PLN151–PLN200
★★★★★ PLN201 and above

RESTAURANTS
American
Hard Rock Cafe ★★★
Virtually identical to all Hard Rock Cafes the world over, but that's not necessarily a bad thing. It offers one of the best burgers in town and is consistently reliable.
Złote Tarasy shopping centre, Złota 59.
Tel: 022 222 0700.

Asian
Asia Tasty ★
One of the very few places where Caucasians are in the minority, the local Vietnamese community rates this place highly: decent food at great prices.
pl. Żelaznej Bramy 1.

Wook ★
Underneath the Marriott you will find the best-value Chinese food in Warsaw. Admittedly, the portions aren't large, but at PLN10 for a main course and side dish you can afford to have two.
al. Jerozolimskie 65/79.

Fusion
Sense ★★★
A stunningly good choice, whether you're after excellent food or superb cocktails. Booking is very much recommended for tables, but there's often space at the bar. Also offers the best range of vodka in the city.
ul. Nowy Świat 19.
Tel: 022 826 6570.

Indian
Namaste Clay Oven ★★
Very probably the best Indian restaurant in Poland, found on one of the Old Town's more charming streets. If you like curry, you simply shouldn't miss this place.
ul. Piwna 12/14.
Tel. 022 635 7766.

Palestra offers some of the best pastas and pizzas in the former ghetto

Namaste India ★★
Small and easy to miss, but serves superb curries that cost less than some places charge for just the rice. Good selection of vegetarian dishes. Essential budget dining and highly recommended.
ul. Nowogrodzka 15.

International
Atrio ★★★★
Excellent international food served by well-trained staff. Conveniently located within 100m (110yds) of three major hotels but well worth travelling across town to get to.
al. Jana Pawła II 23.
Tel: 022 653 9600.
99 ★★★★
Recently renovated and right back to its best as far as the food is concerned. The steak is particularly good, and makes the below-average service more tolerable.
al. Jana Pawła II 23.
Tel: 022 620 1999.

Italian
Na Prowincji ★★
A good choice for budget dining in the Old Town. Quality pasta and pizzas at excellent prices. Wash them down with cheap but very acceptable carafes of wine.
ul. Nowomiejska 10.
Tel: 022 831 9875.
Palestra ★★
Freshly made pasta, very reasonably priced wine and Warsaw's best pizzas cooked in a wood-fired oven. This place is a real little gem.
al. Solidarności 84.
Tel: 022 838 0074.
Bacio ★★★
The kitschest interior in town is home to some of Warsaw's best Italian food. The New Zealand

mussels and peppercorn steak are particularly recommended, and the pasta is excellent.

ul. Wilcza 43.
Tel: 022 626 8303.

St Antonio ★★★★

The décor is very over the top but the location in Saski Park is idyllic – perfect for alfresco dining in the summer. Food can be good but isn't always.

ul. Senatorska 37.
Tel: 022 826 3008.

Lebanese

Samira ★

Hidden down a muddy road that runs along the side of the National Library, Samira serves food that makes the trek from the tram stop well worthwhile, especially at prices this low.

al. Niepodległości 213.

Le Cedre ★★★★

Don't even bother looking at the menu, just order a set meal and the staff will fill literally every centimetre of your table with bowls of delicious food.

al. Solidarności 61.
Tel: 022 670 1166.

Polish

Chłopskie Jadło ★★

The name means 'Farmer's Kitchen', so expect huge portions of simple but excellent food, rustic décor and lashings of *smalec*, beer and vodka. Your best bet for well-priced Polish food.

pl. Konstytucji 1.
Tel: 022 339 1715.

Oberża Pod Czerwonym Wieprzem ★★

The 'Under the Red Hog Inn' is themed on communist-era Poland, with dishes for the 'proletariat' (cheapish) and 'dignitaries and bourgeoisie' (more expensive). Not high class but good fun, especially after a few *sety* (100ml glasses of vodka).

ul. Żelazna 68.
Tel: 022 850 3144.

U Szwejka ★★

A meat-eater's dream and a gastronome's nightmare: country-style dishes that fill your stomach, fuel your muscles and clog your arteries. Try the daily

Chłopskie Jadło: the farmer's kitchen

specials (fresh mussels on Thursday & Friday).
pl. Konstytucji 1.
Tel: 022 339 1710.

Polskie Smaki ★★★
Perhaps not top Polish cuisine, but a good location (just behind ul. Nowy Świat) and very decent food make this a sound choice.
ul. Gałczyńskiego 3.
Tel: 022 826 5967.

Sekret ★★★★
One of the best restaurants in the Old Town but far cheaper than other high-end places nearby. Polish and Hungarian food served in a wonderfully decorated cellar with brilliant Hungarian wine.
ul. Jezuicka 1/3.
Tel: 022 635 7474.

Belvedere ★★★★★
Another contender for the title of finest restaurant in Warsaw. Housed in Royal Łazienki Park's New Orangery, it serves seriously good Polish and European food at seriously high prices.
Enter from ul. Parkowa.
Tel: 022 841 2250.

U Fukiera ★★★★★
Reputedly the best restaurant in Warsaw;
certainly one of the most expensive. The food and service can be excellent, but sometimes are far below what you'd expect for these prices.
Rynek Starego Miasta 27.
Tel: 022 831 1013.

Seafood

Boston Port ★★
Although Warsaw has a dearth of seafood restaurants, Boston Port serves excellent fish. The interior is a little shabby and will never win any awards, but the food wins them regularly.
ul. Okolska 2.
Tel: 022 844 0315.

Sakana ★★★
The finest sushi you'll find anywhere in Poland. Dishes float by on little boats – just grab what you like or ask the chefs to make you something special.
ul. Moliera 4/6.

Tex Mex

Warsaw Tortilla Factory ★★
Warsaw's best choice for Tex-Mex dining. Burritos baked on-site and filled with spicy ingredients.
Live music several nights a week and great staff all the time.
Corner of ul. Poznańska & ul. Wilcza.
Tel: 022 621 8622.

Vegetarian

Greenway ★
The complete opposite of McDonald's in every way apart from the food being cheap, the locations numerous and the service fast.
Locations include ul. Hoża 54, ul. Krucza 23/31, ul. Szpitalna 6 & ul. Świętokrzyska 30.

Vega ★
Vegetarian food and the best value for money in Warsaw: around PLN8 for the set lunch menu!
al. Jana Pawła II 36c; enter from al. Solidarności. Very hard to find – walk through the car park next to Kino Femina and it's straight ahead of you.

CAFÉS

Café culture has only just arrived in Warsaw but it is making up for lost time: almost every street corner has a coffee shop catering to the newly

Food and drink

acquired caffeine addictions of Varsovians. It's a pity about the 'pay at the counter then hang about waiting for your coffee' routine most of them use. Some of the older-style cafés are worth a visit too. Most of these places open at either 8am or 9am and close at about 8pm or 9pm.

6/12
Good café with a superb interior. There is an extensive range of energising/relaxing health drinks. The café au lait is particularly enjoyable and some of the food is as well, but everything's a little pricey.
ul. Żurawia 6/12.

Blikle Café
A Warsaw institution and where Charles de Gaulle used to buy doughnuts when he was in the city. Classic interior and a menu that's guaranteed to shatter any diet.
ul. Nowy Świat 33.

Cafe Bristol
The ideal choice if you aren't paying (a cup of tea costs PLN18). The décor is absolutely

MILK BARS

The *Bar Mleczny* (Milk Bars) are one of the last remnants of the communist era. Set up in the 1950s, they now survive thanks to government (and municipal) subsidies. On the menu are old-fashioned Polish classics but mainly without meat (meat dishes are not eligible for subsidies). Milk bars are very popular with pensioners and students but also attract anybody who wants cheap, home-cooked food: a three-course meal costs about PLN10. The best, but most expensive, is **Uniwersytecki** (*al. Krakowskie Przedmieście 20*). **Prasowy** (*ul. Marszałkowska 10/16*) and **Złota Kurka** (*ul. Marszałkowska 55/73*) are among the other places where there's a fighting chance you won't get food poisoning. Don't expect any staff to speak any language other than Polish, but a bad-tempered glare is usually the limit of their communication anyway. You queue twice: once to order and pay; then again to collect your winnings.

classic, straight out of the 1930s – Warsaw's heyday. Gorgeous fittings are set off by a black and white colour scheme: timeless and delightfully executed.
Krakowskie Przedmieście 42/44.

Chłodna 25
Alternative café-bar, but thankfully has no 'ironic' mullet haircuts or loud discussions about what Sartre really meant. Cheap, eccentric, housed in an architectural gem and utterly unmissable.
ul. Chłodna 25.

Coffeeheaven
The coffee is never truly out of this world but is always good, as are the sandwiches, wraps and muffins. While in the city you will never be far from a Coffeeheaven.
32 locations including the station, the airport & all major shopping centres.

Coffee Karma
Pretentious crowd (laptops in the mornings and Kafka novels in the afternoons) and rather inconsistent service, but it does make a good cup of coffee, eventually.
pl. Zbawiciela 3/5.

Greencoffee
Decent coffee, pleasant décor and good locations. Some people complain about the ciabattas, but the

breakfast baguettes
are a winner.
*ul. Marszałkowska 84/92,
ul. Piękna 18 & ul.
Bracka 16.*

Kawka

A coffee house rather
than a coffee shop.
Comfortable sofas, odd
photographs, home-
made cakes and rather
good coffee make the
place very much
recommended.
ul. Koszykowa 30.

Między Nami

A café so good it's
usually full, but it's
worth waiting for a
table. Offers a decent
selection of light bites
and small meals. Also
serves alcohol (unlike
most cafés).
ul. Bracka 20.

Starbucks

Yes, Starbucks is here too.
And it is almost exactly
the same as all the others
across the planet. You
may think that a good
thing or a bad thing.
*Nowy Świat 62 and
Solidarności 68a & 82.*

BARS

Warsaw has no central
drinking district but it
does offer a very wide

Uniwersytecki milk bar: a culinary experience

choice: everything from
seedy drinking dens to
exclusive establishments
stuffed with wannabe
supermodels and
gentlemen used to
buying anything they
desire. Polish licensing
laws allow bars to open
any time they want; few

places shut much before
midnight during the
week, later on Friday
and Saturday.

Bierhalle

Microbrewery beer
(brewed in their flagship
location at Arkadia
shopping centre), and

particularly good beer too. Always busy, but it's worth waiting for a table.
ul. Nowy Świat 64.

Club Capitol

A stunning venue that shows what a designer with some imagination and a large budget can achieve. Meanwhile, the crowd matches the venue, with designer clothes and cash aplenty.
ul. Marszałkowska 115.

Der Elefant

Good location, a pleasant conservatory, cheap beer and reasonably priced simple solid food make this place an ideal watering hole if you're in the area.
pl. Bankowy 1.

Ice Bar

Ensures the vodka is at the correct temperature by keeping the air temperature at −8 degrees and serving it in shot glasses made of ice, while you chill on chairs made of ice.
Panska 61.

Jimmy Bradleys

One of Warsaw's best pubs is hidden away on the ground floor of an office block. It offers good drinks and real pub grub. It also shows British sports via Warsaw's largest satellite dish.
ul. Sienna 39.

Kwadrat

Half café, half bar, but with a fridge full of the finest beers on offer anywhere in Warsaw. If you like unpasteurised beer, you'll love the Ciechan, Dawne and Mazowieckie.
ul. Poznańska 7.

Many consider Porto Praga to be the best bar on the right bank of the Vistula

Lolek

The middle of Pole Mokotowskie Park is where you'll find one of Warsaw's better beer halls, reasonable beer and lots of barbecued food.
ul. Rokitnicka 20.

Łysy Pingwin

The 'Bald Penguin' is owned by a Swedish Buddhist and is popular with laid-back artsy types who enjoy good beer, conversation and the occasional 'happening'.
ul. Ząbkowska 11.

Metal Bar

By far the best place in the Old Town to get a drink. There are only seven tables inside, but the bar stocks more than 320 types of alcoholic drink.
Old Town Square 8.

Panorama

Perched on the 40th floor of the Marriott Hotel, this is the highest bar in the city and has drink prices to match, but the view is priceless.
al. Jerozolimskie 65/79.

Paparazzi

One of Warsaw's first cocktail bars and, after its recent renovation, still one of the very best. The crowd is smart and monied but attitude-free; the place is swish and stylish.
ul. Mazowiecka 12.

Platinum

This spacious club has a superb interior, reasonable music, a well-heeled crowd and good drinks. This place is definitely worth checking out, assuming you can get in and can afford the prices.
ul. Fredry 6.

Porto Praga

A stunningly good new venue located in less-visited Praga. By far the best bar on the right-hand side of the Vistula, and arguably the best bar in the entire city.
ul. Stefana Okrzei 23.

Przejście dla Pieszych

The best place to get a drink in the New Town. Their house special (Jägermeister, Red Bull and hot vodka) tastes divine, but is a hangover waiting to happen.
ul. Freta 19.

Sense

Slick, smooth and über-cool. Excellent fusion food and the finest vodka in the city, plus deceptively innocent-tasting cocktails that hit you hard. Highly recommended.
ul. Nowy Świat 19.

Warsaw Tortilla Factory

Awesomely dangerous cocktails, tables with built-in beer taps, Sky Sports on TV, regular live music, Tex-Mex food, friendly staff and amiable regulars all under one roof.
ul. Wilcza 46.

A WORD OF WARNING

Polish beer is generally between 6 per cent and 9 per cent alcohol by volume, and spirits are served in 40ml shots rather than the 25ml you may be used to: both of these factors easily lead to getting pie-eyed rather quickly. There is now very little tolerance for drunken tourists behaving badly. The city's 'drunk tank' is by all accounts a very unpleasant place, and an overnight stay awaits if the police take an interest in you. Door staff at many bars are either psychotic or off-duty police, or both; leave them alone and they'll leave you alone (hopefully).

Vodka

The French have wine, the Scots have whisky. Poles have vodka and produce some of the finest types to be found anywhere on the planet. With several hundred different varieties to choose from, it's a safe bet you'll find at least one that suits your taste buds.

Vodka and Poland have a relationship that goes back to at least 1405, a fact proved by the records of Sandomierz court for that year. Back then, distillation was a very tricky process, at least if you wanted a semi-drinkable product anyway. Herbs, fruit or grasses were often added to cover any failings in the process and, from this, flavoured vodka was born. Żubrówka vodka from Białystok is flavoured with Bison grass (there's a piece in every bottle) and can trace its heritage back to the 16th century. Goldwasser from Gdańsk dates from at least the 17th century and each bottle still contains the flakes of gold that give the drink its name.

Poland was famous for its vodka in the 16th century, with exports sent as far afield as England and Moldova, but the distilleries were very much small-scale affairs; in 1580 Poznań alone had 498 distilleries. Only the aristocracy were permitted to produce vodka, and it proved to be a very

good source of revenue. Technological advances led to the three-stage distillation process, and the first industrial distillery was opened in 1782. Polish vodka became the dominant force in the European spirits market, a position strengthened in the mid-19th century when the distillation of potato-based vodka became possible and was maintained until World War I. In 1925 the Polish state gave itself a monopoly on the sale of vodka, and all distilleries were nationalised by the communist government after World War II.

Since the fall of the Iron Curtain in 1989, Poland's vodka industry has been busy regaining its past glory and has done so with considerable success. A number of Polish brands have become among the world leaders. A particularly good example is Wyborowa. The standard triple-distilled version is a very good tipple, but the super-premium 'Single Estate – Exquisite' variety is a thing of true beauty. Made only of grain from a single farm, batch-distilled in the same way as malt whisky and with a bottle designed by Frank Gehry, it is arguably the finest vodka on the planet. Other excellent choices for super-premium clear vodka include Chopin and Belvedere.

Flavoured vodkas remain very popular. Żubrówka is often mixed with apple juice in a cocktail called *Szarlotka* (apple pie). *Wiśniówka* is a cherry vodka with a very sweet taste that hides its strength: it's often 50 per cent alcohol. Made by mixing honey and herbs with vodka, *krupnik* is another favourite for those with a sweet tooth. Herbal vodkas with a dry, bitter taste are also very good; names to look for include Żołądkowa and Soplica (with essence of nuts and fruit, and tasting a little bit like brandy). Starka vodka has been aged; the taste gets better, and the price higher, as the vodka gets older. The drink of choice for those more interested in effect than taste is *spiritus*: 95 per cent alcohol; 99 per cent chance of getting you drunk; and 0 per cent chance of being allowed on a plane because it is highly flammable.

Probably the best place in Warsaw to try the national drink is **Sense** (*Nowy Świat 19*). This bar has 108 vodkas in stock and many more made according to the season, all served in racks of test-tubes that are full of different types so you can find the vodka that is perfect for you. Just watch out for the chilli vodka.

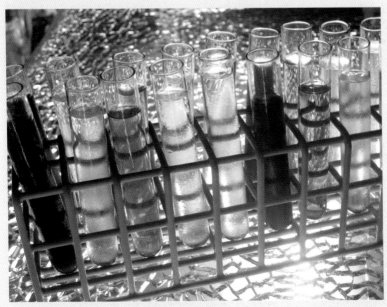

Choose your poison: some of Sense's 108 stock vodkas

Accommodation

Until very recently Warsaw was a destination almost exclusively for business travellers. Several hotels were built in the last decade (and a couple of old ones were extensively renovated), all fighting to attract business people and their corporate expense accounts. This had two side-effects: the lower levels of the market have been largely ignored, and there is an embarrassing surplus of high-end rooms when the business people leave town at weekends.

Prices given are for a standard double/twin room with bathroom but without breakfast and without 7 per cent VAT (unless stated otherwise). Some hotels price their rooms in euros (a few use dollars) but will bill you in złoty at the current rate of exchange. These are standard published rates. Prices tend to be lower at weekends and in summer, sometimes below half the regular price. However, during the week it can be a struggle to find a room for less than PLN300 a night. Book ahead if you don't want to spend large amounts of money.

★	PLN275 or less
★★	PLN276–460
★★★	PLN461–645
★★★★	PLN646–830
★★★★★	PLN831 or more

Boutique hotels

The boutique hotel idea is new to Warsaw, and at the time of writing there are only two in the city. Both of them are excellent.

Le Regina ★★★★★

Housed in a superbly restored row of town houses in the New Town, Le Regina is probably the best place to stay if money is no object. Watch out for the winter weekend specials; prices sometimes drop by 50 per cent. Excellent restaurant. 61 rooms.
ul. Kościelna 12. Tel: 022 531 6000. Email: info@leregina.com. www.leregina.com

Rialto ★★★★★

The interior is an Art Deco masterpiece. Each room is individually designed and finished to the highest possible level. Even the bed sheets are custom-made (from finest Italian linen). 44 rooms.
ul. Wilcza 73. Tel: 022 584 8700. Email: info@rialto.pl. www.hotelrialto.com.pl

Luxury hotels

Apart from the Hyatt, all these hotels are within 3km (1¾ miles) of the

Central Station. All offer high levels of quality with prices to match.

Hilton Warsaw Hotel & Convention Centre ★★★

This hotel opened in mid-2007, making it one of the newest in the city. Excellent design (floor-to-ceiling windows give beautiful views), flawless service and impeccable management make this one of the best hotels in Warsaw. 314 rooms.
ul. Grzybowska 63. Tel: 022 356 5555. Email: reservation.warsaw@ hilton.com.
www.warsaw.hilton.com

Hyatt Regency ★★★

Not in the city centre but between Royal Łazienki Park and Morskie Oko Park. It has some of the biggest rooms in any hotel in the city and all the trappings you'd expect from a five-star hotel. 260 rooms.
ul. Belwederska 23. Tel: 022 558 1234. Email: warsaw.reservations@ hyattintl.com. www. warsaw.regency.hyatt.com

InterContinental ★★★

Yes, the building is supposed to look like that! For some reason, the Warsaw InterContinental only has three legs. But it also has a swimming pool on the 44th floor, probably the best hotel bar in the city (+One bar, which serves a sublime Bloody Mary) and spacious rooms, which all make it a pretty good choice. 405 rooms.
ul. Emilii Plater 49. Tel: 022 328 8888. Email: warsaw@interconti.com.

www.warsaw. intercontinental.com

Marriott ★★★

For two decades this place has dominated Warsaw's skyline and high-end hotel market. Recently, the Marriott has seriously upped its game and is now a great choice. All rooms have been upgraded and renovated but the corner rooms are still the best. 515 rooms.
al. Jerozolimskie 65/79. Tel: 022 630 6306. Email: warsaw-reservation@ marriotthotels.com.
www.marriott.com/wawpl

A room in the Hilton Warsaw Hotel

Novotel Warszawa Centrum ★★★

Recently renovated and large, with the most central location possible. However, apart from the sauna on the 31st floor with a window overlooking Warsaw's city centre, the Novotel is seriously outclassed by the other hotels in this price bracket. 733 rooms.
ul. Marszałkowska 94/98. Tel: 022 621 0271. Email: nov.warszawa@orbis.pl. www.orbisonline.pl

Polonia Palace Hotel ★★★

The façade is the same as the 1913 original, but the rest of the hotel changed during an extended reconstruction. The lobby is now in an impressive glass-topped atrium and the rooms have almost doubled in size. This fine hotel also has an excellent bar (Bojangles). 208 rooms.
al. Jerozolimskie 45. Tel: 022 318 2800. Email: pp.reservation@ syrena.com.pl. www.poloniapalace.com

Radisson SAS Centrum ★★★

A safe choice. The hotel offers rooms with different design themes: Scandinavian, Italian and 'maritime'. The basement gym is one of the best hotel gyms in town. 311 rooms.
ul. Grzybowska 24. Tel: 022 321 8888. Email: reservation.warsaw@ radissonsas.com. www.radissonsas.com

Sheraton Warsaw Hotel ★★★★

A major hub of the expat community and a first-class hotel. Good gym and even better restaurants. The hotel's Someplace Else bar has live music and is popular despite its high prices. 350 rooms.
ul. Prusa 2. Tel: 022 450 6100. Email: warsaw@sheraton.com. www.sheraton.com.pl

Sofitel Victoria Warsaw ★★★★

Superb location on pl. Piłsudskiego and good rooms (particularly the business rooms), but cynics say the best thing about the Victoria is that if you're in it, you can't see how ugly the building is. 341 rooms.
ul. Królewska 11. Tel: 022 657 8011. Email: rez.sof.victoria@orbis.pl. www.orbisonline.pl

The Westin ★★★★

One to avoid if you're

Le Regina: the place to stay if money is no object

afraid of heights: the only way to your room is in glass lifts that whisk you up a glass tube on the side of the building. Decent rooms and excellent deals at weekends. 361 rooms. *al. Jana Pawła II 21. Tel: 022 450 8000. Email: warsaw@westin.com. www.westin.com.pl*

Le Royal Méridien Bristol ★★★★★

Next door to the President's Palace and, according to some people, slightly more luxurious. The hotel was restored in the early 1990s to regain the Art Nouveau style that made it a favourite of the great and the good between the wars. 200 rooms. *ul. Krakowskie Przedmieście 42/44. Tel: 022 551 1000. Email: bristol@lemeridien.com. www.warsaw.lemeridien. com*

Mid-range hotels

There are far fewer to choose from in this price range than in the luxury sector, but these hotels usually receive favourable reviews. All prices here include VAT.

Campanile ★

In the same building as the Kyriad Prestige (which is PLN100 more expensive per night) and the Premiere Classe (PLN80 less per night) is Campanile, probably the best quality-to-cost ratio of the three. Spotless bathrooms and satellite TV in every room. 194 rooms. *ul. Towarowa 2. Tel: 022 582 7200. Email: warszawa@campanile. com.pl. www.campanile.com.pl*

Ibis Hotel – Stare Miasto ★

By far the best choice for mid-range accommodation (and arguably the only decent choice). The Stare Miasto Ibis has an excellent location, just five minutes' walk from the New Town Market Square, but the Warszawa Centrum Ibis is slightly cheaper, less likely to be full and only four tram stops from pl. Zamkowy. 333 rooms. *ul. Muranowska 2. Tel:*

022 310 1000. Email: H3714@accor.com. www.orbis.pl

Ibis Hotel – Warszawa Centrum ★

189 rooms. *al. Solidarności 165. Tel: 022 520 3000. Email: H2894@accor.com. www.orbis.pl*

Agrykola ★★

Nothing special but nothing too unpleasant either. Finding the way in can be tricky. The staff are tolerant and some can even be helpful. The room rate includes breakfast. 26 rooms. *ul. Myśliwiecka 9. Tel: 022 622 9110. Email: recepcja@agrykola-noclegi.pl. www.agrykola-noclegi.pl*

Kyriad Prestige ★★

This is the most luxurious of the three hotels run by the Envergure group and also the most expensive. The extra money buys you things like guest-sized bottles of shampoo, access to the gym and, most importantly, more comfortable beds. 133 rooms. *ul. Towarowa 2. Tel: 022 582 7500. Email:*

warszawa@kyriad
prestige.com.pl. www.
kyriadprestige.com.pl

Budget hotels

Finding anything close to
acceptable for under
PLN200 a night is very
difficult indeed. The two
best choices are fairly
new but also fairly basic.

Etap ★

This hotel is in the
riverside Powiśle district,
which means a bit of
walking but also plenty
of peace and quiet. All
rooms are modern and
clean, with en-suite
bathrooms and cable
television; Wi-Fi is also
available in all the rooms.
Good value for money.
176 rooms.
*ul. Zagórna 1. Tel: 022
745 3660. Email:
H6401@accor.com.
www.orbisonline.pl*

Premiere Classe ★

The most popular one-
star hotel in Warsaw – it's
best to book in advance
or you may be unable to
get a room. All rooms
have a television and en-
suite bathroom.
126 rooms.
ul. Towarowa 2. Tel: 022

*624 0800. Email:
rezerwacjawarszawa@
premiereclasse.com.pl.
www. premiereclasse.
com.pl*

Hostels

All of the older-style
youth hostels are best
avoided unless you want
a very early curfew and
middle-of-the-day
lock-out. These four,
however, are more
modern and spoken of
well by most guests.

Agrykola ★

This is in the same
building as the mid-
price, mid-range and
mid-quality hotel with
the same name. All the
rooms are modern and
have plenty of space. The
hostel has one triple
room, six quadruple
rooms and fifty dorm
beds. Often fully booked.
The room rate includes
breakfast.
*ul. Myśliwiecka 9. Tel:
022 622 9110. Email:
recepcja@agrykola-
noclegi.pl.
www.agrykola-noclegi.pl*

Kanonia ★

Atmospheric and located
on a cobbled street in the

Old Town. There is a
trade-off for that charm:
the rooms are very small
and passers-by can stare
through some of the
windows.
*ul. Jezuicka 2. Tel: 022
635 0676. Email:
hostel@kanonia.pl.
www.kanonia.pl*

Nathan's Villa Hostel ★

Warsaw's best hostel is
run by the same man
who runs Kraków's best
hostel. Owner Nathan
has stayed in many
hostels and learnt exactly
what makes one great.
Now he's put it all into
practice. The only thing
less than excellent is the
number of rooms: just
nineteen of them,
including six doubles and
three quadruple rooms.
*ul. Piękna 24/26. Tel/fax:
022 622 2946. Email:
warsaw@nathansvilla.
com.
www.nathansvilla.com*

Oki Doki ★

This hostel has a good
city-centre location and
has recently been
remodelled so that there
are more private rooms.
There are no numbers on
the rooms; instead, each
has a theme: 'The

Communist Dorm' is a must for all fans of socialist styling. One single room, twenty-one doubles and sixty dorm beds. The room rate includes breakfast.
pl. Dąbrowskiego 3. Tel: 022 826 5112. Email: okidoki@okidoki.pl. www.okidoki.pl

Serviced apartments

If you think you can manage without room service, a porter and even a minibar, a serviced apartment may be a good choice. Prices are per night for the cheapest apartment the company has.

Old Town Apartments ★★

Despite the name, this company has about 50 apartments located in various parts of the city. On offer is everything from one-room studio apartments to 120sq m (1,290sq ft) places that sleep the whole family.
Rynek Starego Miasta 12/14. Tel: 022 820 9227. Email: warsaw@bookaa.net. www.warsawshotel.com

Residence Diana ★★

Chic, swish, sophisticated and utterly beautiful. The complex has English-speaking receptionists around the clock and a laundry service. Of course, this all comes at a price. 46 apartments.
ul. Chmielna 13a. Tel: 022 505 9100. Email: info@residencediana.com. www.residencediana.com

Residence St Andrews Palace ★★★

Luxurious apartments in a wonderfully restored town house. 24 apartments.
ul. Chmielna 30.

Tel: 022 826 46 40. Email: info@residencestandrews. pl. www. residencestandrews.pl

Private rooms

There are a few characters who hang around the Central Station offering private rooms. Some have excellent rooms at great prices; others have dives for silly money. The average is closer to the second of those extremes. Don't part with any money before you've seen the room.

Nathan's Villa: twice voted one of the world's top ten hostels

Practical guide

Arriving

Visas

Poland has now fully implemented the Schengen agreement and therefore citizens of other Schengen zone nations do not need to show their passports when entering Poland. However, neither the UK nor Ireland has to date joined Schengen, therefore all British and Irish visitors do need valid passports to enter Poland. Citizens of all other nations need passports and many (including Chinese, Indians, Russians, Jamaicans and South Africans) also need visas. Polish visas are normally only issued in the country where the applicant is a permanent resident.

By air

Most visitors arrive by air and so are welcomed by Port Lotniczy im.

Fryderyka Chopina (Warsaw Fryderyk Chopin airport), better known by its former name of Okęcie airport. After several years of delays, there are now two terminals forming a single building: Terminal One (on the left, opened in 1992) and Terminal Two (on the right, opened mid-2008). In doubt as to which you need? Check which number your check-in desk is: those starting with 'one' are in Terminal One and those starting with 'two' are in Terminal Two.

Bus No 175 runs from the airport to the city centre. Ticket inspectors like this bus, so buy a ticket (*billety*) from the kiosks on the ground floor of the airport and validate it in the machine on the bus – unstamped tickets are not valid. Pickpockets also love this bus. Unless your budget is really tight, it's best to spend a bit more and get a taxi.

Warsaw airport's shiny new Terminal Two

The departures hall of Warsaw airport's Terminal One

The arrivals hall is home to men with home-made ID cards who will offer you a taxi. Avoid them unless you want to pay five to ten times more than the PLN30 to PLN40 a ride to the city centre should cost. Walk outside the terminal and take a taxi from one of the three officially approved companies: MPT, Sawa and Merc. In the unlikely event there are no taxis, look for the three men wearing brightly coloured jackets bearing the name of one of those companies; they will radio for a taxi.

A second airport is being developed at a former military airfield in Modlin, 40km (25 miles) from Warsaw. Completion is currently scheduled for 2011, a mere six years behind the original completion date. The airport will focus on low-cost airlines but until the planned rail connection to Warsaw is built, getting there won't be much fun.

By car

If arriving by car, the best idea is to drive to a guarded car park (*Parking Strzeżony*) and leave your car there. Driving in Warsaw is not advisable: the average Varsovian driver has no patience at all, an unshakeable faith in their ability to drive like Steve McQueen, an almost complete disregard for the laws of road traffic and physics, and a talent for driving at high speed through gaps slightly too narrow for a car. The biggest difficulty for novice drivers in Warsaw (apart from Varsovian drivers) is trams. Unless traffic lights are against them, trams always have the right of way. They also have very bad brakes and can't swerve to avoid you. Never overtake a tram that is stationary in the road at a passenger stop as people will be getting on and off.

By train

Warsaw Central Station (*al. Jerozolimskie 54*) has so many subterranean passageways that getting lost in them is to be expected. Keep an eye out for the signposts and when in doubt just follow the crowd. The ticket hall is on the ground floor and has a couple of kiosks, a café, a pharmacy and a *kantor* (bureau de change, which offers less than competitive rates; better value can be found elsewhere). Very few of the railway staff will speak any language other than Polish, so the easiest way to buy a train ticket is to write on a piece of paper the name of the place you want to go to and the time the train leaves Warsaw (timetables are yellow for departures and white for arrivals), *klasa* (class) 1 or 2, and hand the piece of paper to a ticket clerk.

Climate

Warsaw's climate is one of extremes. Summer may bring roasting heat with occasional heavy downpours, while the frost is quite severe in January and February; lately, however, winters have been light without excessive snow or rainfall. Spring and autumn are seasons of strong wind, while autumn shares with winter a lack of strong sunlight.

Customs regulations

If you are arriving from the EU, there are no limits for duty-paid goods for personal use. If coming from outside the EU, your limits are (per adult): 200

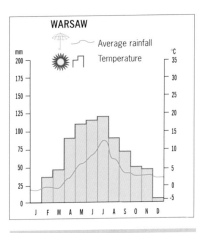

WARSAW

Average rainfall
Temperature

J F M A M J J A S O N D

WEATHER CONVERSION CHART

25.4mm = 1 inch
°F = 1.8 × °C + 32

cigarettes or 100 cigarillos or 50 cigars or 250g of tobacco; 1 litre of spirits or 2 litres of wine, and 75cc of perfume. Despite Poland being in the EU, most EU member states will not allow you to bring more than 200 cigarettes back from Poland.

Nothing made before 1945 can be taken out of Poland without a special permit. This rule does not only apply to Polish works of art and books: it applies to anything made before 1945, regardless of where it was produced.

Driving

Most Polish roads were built for light local use only and are completely unsuitable for the volume (and weight) of today's traffic. Very few roads have more than one lane in either direction: you will be expected to drive on the hard shoulder (where pedestrians walk) so as to make half of a third lane when somebody wants to overtake you. Seeing four cars side-by-side across these three lanes is common, five or even six can be seen occasionally. Official estimates used to class more than 95 per cent of roads as being in need of immediate replacement (a problem solved by no longer releasing official estimates). Poland leads the EU in both number of road traffic accidents and resulting deaths. Wearing seat belts whenever they are fitted is a legal requirement.

Poland has strict blood alcohol limits when driving: 0.2mg of alcohol per millilitre of blood, so even one beer can put you over the limit. Being caught at above 0.4mg/ml results in your car being confiscated, permanently.

The speed limit is 50km/h (30mph) in cities, 90km/h (55mph) outside built-up areas, 110km/h (68mph) on dual carriageways and 130km/h (80mph) on motorways.

Your car must carry a red warning triangle, first-aid kit, replacement bulbs and a national identity sticker. You must have your passport, car insurance and registration documents (originals, not copies) and driving licence (if your licence is non-EU, an international permit is a good idea and you must obtain a Polish licence after being in Poland for six months).

Foreigners must pay fines for any road traffic offences to police on the spot and in cash; offering bribes is now

CONVERSION TABLE

FROM	TO	MULTIPLY BY
Inches	Centimetres	2.54
Feet	Metres	0.3048
Yards	Metres	0.9144
Miles	Kilometres	1.6090
Acres	Hectares	0.4047
Gallons	Litres	4.5460
Ounces	Grams	28.35
Pounds	Grams	453.6
Pounds	Kilograms	0.4536
Tons	Tonnes	1.0160

To convert back, for example, from centimetres to inches, divide by the number in the third column.

MEN'S SUITS

UK	36	38	40	42	44	46	48
Rest of Europe	46	48	50	52	54	56	58
USA	36	38	40	42	44	46	48

DRESS SIZES

UK	8	10	12	14	16	18
France	36	38	40	42	44	46
Italy	38	40	42	44	46	48
Rest of Europe	34	36	38	40	42	44
USA	6	8	10	12	14	16

MEN'S SHIRTS

UK	14	14.5	15	15.5	16	16.5	17
Rest of Europe	36	37	38	39/40	41	42	43
USA	14	14.5	15	15.5	16	16.5	17

MEN'S SHOES

UK	7	7.5	8.5	9.5	10.5	11
Rest of Europe	41	42	43	44	45	46
USA	8	8.5	9.5	10.5	11.5	12

WOMEN'S SHOES

UK	4.5	5	5.5	6	6.5	7
Rest of Europe	38	38	39	39	40	41
USA	6	6.5	7	7.5	8	8.5

a bad idea. Headlights must be switched on at all times year-round. Levels of car-related crime are falling but are still high enough to make guarded car parks a good idea. Foreign licence plates attract attention from both the police and thieves.

Electricity

Poland uses 220 volts, 50 cycle AC, and standard two-pin continental plugs. Visitors requiring 110 volts will need a voltage transformer.

Embassies

Australia

ul. Nowogrodzka 11. Tel: 022 521 3444. www.australia.pl. Open: 9am–5pm.

Canada

ul. Matejki 1/5. Tel: 022 584 3100/31. www.canada.pl. Open: 8.30am–4.30pm.

Finland

ul. Chopina 4/8. Tel: 022 598 9500. Open: 8am–4pm.

Ireland

ul. Mysia 5. Tel: 022 849 6633. www.irlandia.pl. Open: Mon–Fri 9am–1pm.

Japan

ul. Szwoleżerów 8. Tel: 022 696 5005. www.pl.emb-japan.go.jp

New Zealand

al. Ujazdowskie 51. Tel: 022 521 0500. www.nzembassy.pl

South Africa

ul. Koszykowa 54, 6th floor. Tel: 022 625 6228/6233/7239. www.southafrica.pl. Open: 9am–noon.

Sweden

ul. Bagatela 3. Tel: 022 640 8900. www.swedishembassy.pl. Open: 9am–1pm.

United Kingdom

al. Róży 1. Tel: 022 311 0000. www.britishembassy.pl. Open: Mon–Thur 8.30am–5pm, Fri 8.30am–2.30pm.

The New Zealand Embassy building

The House under Eagles on ul. Jasna, a branch of BPH bank

United States

al. Ujazdowskie 29/31. Tel: 022 504 2000. www.usinfo.pl. Citizens' Services open: Mon–Fri 9am–noon.

Emergency telephone numbers

Ambulance: *999*
Fire Brigade: *998*
Police: *997*
Emergency services from a mobile phone: *112*
There are few, if any, English-speaking operators at these numbers.

Health

In theory, any citizen from a European Economic Area (EEA) country who has a valid European Health Insurance Card (EHIC) is entitled to free healthcare in Poland. However, the Polish state healthcare system is infamously overstretched and underfunded, the bureaucracy involved in using it is daunting, and some state hospitals refuse point-blank to assist holders of the EHIC unless payment is made in cash in advance. Going private is a much better option. A consultation normally costs in the region of PLN100, and having a simple fracture (ankle, wrist, etc) put in a cast is about PLN500. Reputable clinics with English-speaking doctors include:
Damian Hospital, *ul. Wałbrzyska 46. Tel: 022 566 2222. Open: 24-hour service. Also at ul. Foksal 3/5. www.damian.pl*

(*Cont. on p182*)

Language

Despite first appearances, the Polish language does have vowels. Be glad you're in Warsaw: if you were visiting Gdańsk, you might go to Wrzeszcz; if in the mountains, Szczyrk is nicer to visit than to say. However, what seems to be a tongue-twisting hiss of esses and zeds is actually a completely phonetic language.

a	the 'a' in ant
ą	a nasal 'ong'
c	the 'ts' in sits
ć and ci	the soft 'ch' in cheese
cz	the hard 'ch' in church
dz	the 'ds' in heads
drz and d	the 'j' in jam
e	the 'e' in hen
ę	a nasal 'eng'
h and ch	the Scottish 'ch' of loch
i	the 'ee' in seen
j	the 'y' in yes
ł	the 'w' in wait
ń	the middle 'n' of companion
o	the 'o' in top
ó and u	the 'oo' in boot
r	the 'r' in rolled
rz and ź	the 's' in pleasure, unless rz follows a consonant, in which case it's the 'sh' in harsh
s	the 's' in sit
z	the 'sh' in shut
ś and si	a soft 'sh'
w	the 'v' in vine
y	the 'i' in sit
ż and zi	a soft 's' in leisure

b, d, f, g, k, l, m, n, p, t, x and **z** are all the same as in English

Numbers
Pronunciation is in brackets.

0	*zero*	(zero)
1	*jeden*	(yeden)
2	*dwa*	(dva)
3	*trzy*	(tshi)
4	*cztery*	(chteri)
5	*pięć*	(p'yench)
6	*sześć*	(sheysh-ch)
7	*siedem*	(sh'edem)
8	*osiem*	(oshem)
9	*dziewięć*	(djev'yench)
10	*dziesięć*	(djeshench)

Basic phrases
Pronunciation is in brackets.

Hi/Bye	*Cześć* (cheshch)	
Good day (formal)	*Dzień dobry* (djYen dobree)	
Good evening (formal)	*Dobry wieczór* (dobree ve'yechore)	
Goodbye	*Do widzenia* (do vidzen'ya)	
Good night	*Dobranoc* (dobrranots)	
Yes	*tak* (tak)	
No	*nie* (n'yeh)	
Thank you	*Dziękuje* (djyen'kooyeh)	
Please	*Prosz* (prrosheh)	
You're welcome	*Proszę bardzo* (prrosheh bahr'dzo)	
Excuse me	*Przepraszam* (psheprasham)	
Do you speak English?	*Czy pan mówi po angielsku?* (cuh pan movee po ange'elsku)	
I don't understand	*Nie rozumiem* (n'yeh rro'zoom 'yem)	
I do not speak Polish	*Nie mówię po polsku* (n'yeh movee po polsku)	

I'm lost	*Zabłądziłem* (masc.) (zahbwonjeewem) *Zabłądziłam* (fem.) (zahbwonjeewahm)	**The bill, please**	*poproszę rachunek* (po'prrosheh ra'hoo'nek)
I don't know	*Nie wiem* (nye vyem)	**Where is the... ?**	*Gdzie jest... ?* (g'jay yest)
Nice to meet you	*Bardzo mi miło* (barrdso mee meewo)	**Bank**	*bank* (bank)
What is your name?	*Jak się nazywasz?* (yahk shen nah'zeevash)	**Bakery**	*piekarnia* (p'yeh'karrn'ya)
My name is...	*Nazywam się...* (nah'zeevahm shen...)	**Cash machine**	*bankomat* (bahnkomaht)
How are things?	*Co słychać?* (tsoh swe'hatch)	**Chemist**	*apteka* (apteka)
What's this/that?	*Co to jest?* (tso to yeast)	**Post office**	*poczta* (pochta)
How much is this?	*Ile to kosztuje?* (eeleh to kosh'tooyeh)	**Railway station**	*dworzec* (d'vodjets)
		Toilet	*toaleta* (toahleta)
I'd like...	*poproszę...* (po'prrosheh)	**Tourist office**	*biuro turystyczne* (bee'ooro toorristichne)
Beer	*piwo* (peevo)	**Left**	*lewo* (lehvo)
Coffee	*kawa* (kava)	**Right**	*prawo* (prahvo)
Apple juice	*sok jabłkowy* (sok jab'kovi)	**Here**	*tu* (too)
Orange juice	*sok pomarańczowy* (sok pomoranchovi)	**Over there**	*tam* (tam)
		Straight on	*prosto* (prrosto)
Tea	*herbata* (herbata)	**Yesterday**	*wczoraj* (vchoray)
Sparkling water	*woda gazowana* (vodda gazovana)	**Today**	*dzisiaj* (jeeshay)
Still water	*woda niegazowana* (vodda n'yehgazovana)	**Tomorrow**	*jutro* (yootro)
		Entrance	*wejście* (weysh'thye)
Red wine	*wino czerwony* (veeno chair'voni)	**Exit**	*wyjście* (wysh'thye)
White wine	*wino biały* (veeno bee'awi)	**Platform**	*peron* (peron)
A lot	*dużo* (do'jo)	**Tram stop**	*przystanek autobusowy* (pshees'tahnek ahw'toboosove)
A little	*mało* (ma'wo)	**Train**	*pociąg* (potshiong)
Good/Bad	*dobry/zły* (dobrree/zwi)	**Normal ticket**	*bilet normalny* (beelet normalnee)
Hot/Cold	*gorący/zimny* (gorontsi/zimni)	**Student ticket**	*bilet studencki* (beelet stoodentskey)
Cheers!	*Na zdrowie!* (nah zdrovie)	**Daily ticket**	*bilet dzienny* (bee'let djyen'ni)
		City map	*plan miasta* (plan me'asta)
		Timetable	*rozkład jazdy* (roz'kwad yaz'di)
		Postcard	*pocztówka* (poch'toov'kah)
		Postage stamp	*znaczek* (znachek)

LIM Medical Center, *al. Jerozolimskie 65/79 (Marriott Hotel). Tel: 022 458 7000. Open: Mon–Fri 7am–9pm, Sat 8am–8pm, Sun 9am–6pm. www.cmlim.pl*
Lux-Med, *ul. Racławicka 132 b. Tel: 022 332 2888. Open: 24-hour service. www.luxmed.pl*
Medicover D-4, *ul. Bitwy Warszawskiej 1920 r. 18. Tel: 041 19596. www.medicover.pl*

Media

The best English-language publication in Poland is *In Your Pocket*. The Warsaw edition has superb detail and honest reviews written in an enjoyably entertaining style. Download it from *www.inyourpocket.com* or pick up a copy at any hotel. The *New Warsaw Express* is a free fortnightly publication with general news about Poland and information about events; there is also a weekly version available via email. The *Warsaw Voice* is a weekly newspaper with general news and a history nearly two

The entrance to an Old Town chemist

decades long. The *Insider* is a monthly guide to shopping and facials in Warsaw. It also has reviews and offers pearls of wisdom, such as curry being the 'right choice' in an Indian restaurant. The *Warsaw Business Journal* is the best weekly English-language publication about business because it's the only one. *The Visitor* is badly written rubbish that lures the unwary into the tourist traps that advertise in it.

Money matters

The currency of Poland is the złoty. Usually written as 'zł' or 'PLN', it is divided into 100 groszy. Złoty notes come in 10, 20, 50, 100 and 200 denominations; coins in 1, 2 and 5 złoty and 1, 2, 5, 10, 20 and 50 groszy. Small shops generally have very little change and dislike large notes; many taxi drivers are very reluctant to give change. Credit cards are now widely accepted in Warsaw.

Changing money

Kantors (bureaux de change) offer better rates than banks and have far shorter queues. Few places, if any, will change Scottish or Irish pounds. Cashpoints (ATMs) are plentiful: just look for the word *bankomat*. Unfortunately, only banks change traveller's cheques; expect a queue and reams of paperwork, but you will be free from the hazards of carrying large amounts of cash and, in the event of loss or theft, you will be quickly refunded (make sure you note down the numbers of your traveller's cheques and keep this note in a separate place). *Thomas Cook Traveller's Cheque Refund. Open: 24-hour service – report loss or theft within 24 hours. Tel: +44 1733 318950 (see pp186–7 for information about how to reverse charges).*

Opening hours

Most shops are open from 10am until at least 6pm on weekdays and until 3pm on Saturdays. Shopping centres, however, are usually open until 8pm seven days a week. Shops that open 24 hours a day are called *sklep nocny*; ask at your hotel where the nearest one is. A recently introduced law bans shops from opening on 12 days of the year, most of which are Catholic feast days.

Public holidays

1 January – New Year's Day
March/April – Easter Sunday and
   Monday
1 May – May Day
3 May – Constitution Day
May/June – Pentecost
May/June – Corpus Christi
15 August – Assumption Day
1 November – All Saints' Day
11 November – Independence Day
25–26 December – Christmas

Public transport

Warsaw's public transport network is very cheap and fairly efficient. The same tickets can be used on trams and buses as well as on the underground. Tickets can be bought from most kiosks

Warsaw's oldest tram

and are available as single-use tickets (currently PLN2.40) or for a certain amount of time: 24-hour tickets are PLN7.20; three-day tickets PLN12; and one-week tickets PLN24. A surcharge applies for night buses, which run between midnight and 6am, but it is far better to take a taxi at those times; night buses can be rather unsafe. A surcharge of PLN0.50 is put on tickets bought from drivers of trams and buses, if any are available. Single-use tickets must be inserted into the machines by the bus and tram doors as soon as you enter; time-period tickets must be stamped once by those machines and then they are valid.

If you are caught without a ticket you will be given a fine of PLN84. The full fine is PLN120, but as a foreigner you must pay on the spot and so can claim the 30 per cent reduction for paying

(*Cont. on p186*)

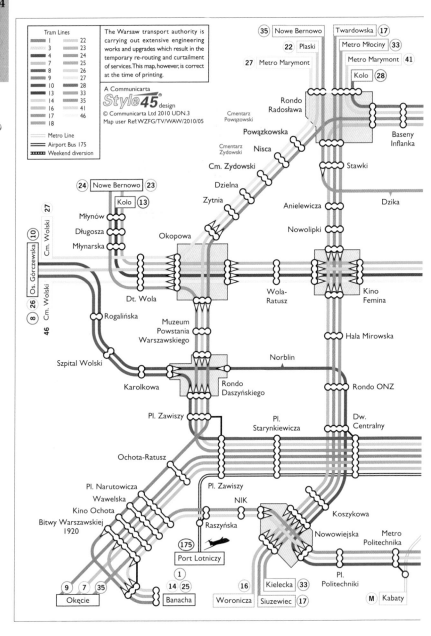

The Warsaw transport authority is carrying out extensive engineering works and upgrades which result in the temporary re-routing and curtailment of services. This map, however, is correct at the time of printing.

Tram Lines

1	22
3	23
4	24
7	25
8	26
9	27
10	28
13	33
14	35
16	41
17	46
18	

Metro Line
Airport Bus 175
Weekend diversion

A Communicarta
Style45 design
© Communicarta Ltd 2010 UDN.3
Map user Ref:WZFG/TV/WAW/2010/05

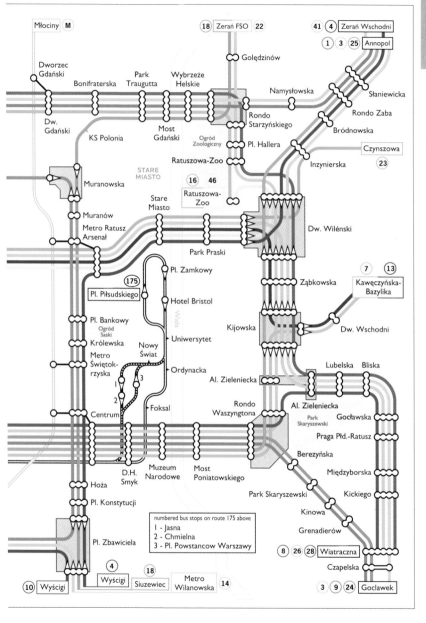

within seven days. Since 1 July 2004 there has been no requirement to buy a ticket for oversized luggage. However, it is not unheard of for ticket inspectors to try to collect fines for this 'offence' anyway; just laugh at them. Students younger than 26 who have a valid International Student Identity Card (ISIC) are entitled to a 48 per cent reduction on all tickets (*bilety ulgowy*); children under the age of six and adults over the age of seventy travel for free if they have ID proving their age.

Taxis

With the exception of the mafia-run unlicensed cabs at the airport, Warsaw taxis are generally honest and fairly cheap. That said, only take cabs that have the name and number of a company on their roof sign, because the 'independents' tend to take tourists for a ride in more ways than one. Hotel taxis are almost all expensive luxury cars, but these cars are paid for by the ultra-high fares they charge. The best option is to phone for a taxi; the staff at any good bar or restaurant should happily do this for you. Despite being state-run, **MPT** (*tel: 022 19191*) is the best company. It has English-speaking operators and a huge fleet of cars, making it reliable and easy to use. Other good options include **Halo** (*tel: 022 19623*), **Merc** (*tel: 022 677 7777*) and **Ele** (*tel: 022 811 1111*). **Wawa** (*tel: 022 29644*) is 10 per cent cheaper but often arrives 20 minutes later than

promised, so avoid using them when you have a plane or train to catch.

Sustainable tourism

Thomas Cook is a strong advocate of ethical and fairly traded tourism and believes that the travel experience should be as good for the places visited as it is for the people who visit them. That's why we firmly support The Travel Foundation, a charity that develops solutions to help improve and protect holiday destinations, their environment, traditions and culture. To find out what you can do to make a positive difference to the places you travel to and the people who live there, please visit *www.thetravelfoundation.org.uk*

Telephones

Public phones are found in many places, but working public phones are another story. Phonecards with various amounts of credit are sold at newsagents and post offices. There are two different types of card: chip and magnetic strip.

To make an international call, dial *00* followed by the country code:
Australia *61*
Canada and the USA *1*
New Zealand *64*
UK *44*
and then dial the foreign number (without the first *0*).

To reverse charges on an international call, first call the country direct number:
UK *(00 800) 441 1144 or 441 1202,*

USA *(00 800) 111 1111 or 111 1112.*
Tell the operator the number you want
and request reversed charges.

Mobile phones

Polish mobile phones are the same
Global System for Mobile (GSM)
900/1800 and third-generation
Universal Mobile Telecommunications
System (UMTS) as the rest of Europe.
GSM 1900 and CDMA handsets will
not work here. There are no mobile
phone rental shops in Warsaw, but
new GSM 900/1800 handsets start
at PLN150.

Internet

Most hotels and some bars and
restaurants have Wi-Fi hotspots.
Internet cafés are scattered throughout
the city; several at Warsaw Central
Station are open 24 hours a day. A
particularly good choice, and popular
with foreigners, is **Casablanca** (*ul.
Krakowskie Przedmieście 4/6*).

Thomas Cook

Thomas Cook services in Poland are
available through Neckermann travel
shops. There is a branch in Warsaw at
ul. Dubois 9 (*tel: 022 536 9898*) and
another at pl. Konstytucji 4 (*tel: 022
622 4022*). You cannot cash traveller's
cheques at these branches, but they will
offer emergency assistance.

Time

Warsaw is in the Central Europe Time
zone (CET), one hour ahead of

Greenwich Mean Time. When it's noon
in Warsaw, it's midnight in Auckland,
9pm in Sydney, noon in Cape Town,
11am in London, 6am in New York,
midnight in Chicago and 11pm the
previous day in Los Angeles. All those
times vary by one hour due to the
differing international usage of daylight
saving time (which is used in Warsaw
from 25 March to 28 October).

Toilets

Public toilets are few and far between.
All charge 1 or 2 złoty and spend
virtually none of that money on
cleaning products. Restaurants and bars
have finally stopped charging customers
for the use of their toilets. Poland has
a strange way of marking toilet doors:
a triangle for the men's; a circle for
the women's; a circle and a triangle
together is for a unisex toilet (usually
just one cubicle).

Travellers with disabilities

Facilities for people with disabilities are
very slowly getting better, but much
remains to be done. The newer hotels
and all the high-end hotels do have
facilities, but few bars or restaurants
do. Most of the main tourist sights
have a wheelchair ramp but little else.
Toilets for people with disabilities are
mainly found only in four- or five-star
hotels and in some of the more
modern public buildings. MPT, Ele,
Merc and Sawa (*see opposite*) all offer
taxis suitable for people with
disabilities.

Index

Acknowledgements

Thomas Cook Publishing wishes to thank the photographers, picture libraries and other organisations, to whom the copyright belongs, for the photographs in this book.

SYLWESTER BRAUN 14
DREAMSTIME 1 (Tomasz Bidermann)
ANDREW ESPINOSA 102, 103
FLICKR 27 (access.denied); 155 (Giam)
PENELOPE GRACE 178
HILTON WARSAW 169
JAN JAGIELSKI 131
JEWISH HISTORY INSTITUTE ARCHIVE 72
WOJCIECH KRYŃSKI 45
LE REGINA 170
NATHAN'S VILLA 173
NATIONAL PHILHARMONIC ARCHIVE 21
OLYMPIC CASINO 149
POLITYKA MAGAZINE NR 2 (2486) 13
MACIEJ SKOCZEŃ 127
SYLWIA STREBSKA 19, 24, 30, 31, 34, 39, 49, 53, 55, 56, 69, 75, 78, 82, 86, 87, 88, 91, 94, 97, 99, 100, 106, 110, 113, 115, 120, 121, 125, 135, 137, 145, 160, 163
CHRISTIAN SWINDELLS 28, 60, 61, 68, 77, 79, 90, 93, 98, 107, 159, 164, 167
TRAMWAJE WARSZAWSKIE SP.Z.O.O. 183
ALEX WEBBER 10, 32, 35, 43, 50, 85, 148
WIKIMEDIA COMMONS 51 (Vindur); 63, 147 (Gophi); 133, 138, 140 (Wojsyl); 139 (Semu); 141 (Ejdzej); 142 (HuBar); 143 (Polimerek); 156 (Stako); 174, 175 (Foma)
KRZYSZTOF WOJCIECHOWSKI 23
WORLD PICTURES/PHOTOSHOT 41
EWA ZIÓŁKOWSKA 151

Hachette Livre Poland would like to thank the following individuals and institutions who have given their permission for the publication of photographs that they own:
Grzegorz Wilk; Krystyna Bartosik – the National Ethnographic Museum; Kamila Gawędzka – Fabryka Trzciny Artistic Centre; Agnieszka Horbaczewska – Santorini; Kuba Kamiński – Czuły Barbarzyńca; Agnieszka Koperniak – Muranów Cinema; Sebastian Madejski – Zachęta Gallery; Ewa Magiera – the Home Office of the Director of Citizens' Platform (PO); Katarzyna Michalak – the Jan III Sobieski Hotel; Bartosz Nagórny – Warsaw Underground; Dionizy Piątkowski – Director of the Era Jazz Festival; Paweł Pokora – the Dramatyczny Theatre; Małgorzata Potocka and Beata Trochimiuk – Sabat Theatre; Wojciech Rohoziński – Director of the F Chopin Airport; Sylwia Stawska – the Sheraton Hotel; Jolanta Tuchowska; Krzysztof Wojciechowski; Ewa Ziółkowska – Warsaw Zoo; Katarzyna Żebrowska – Luksfera Gallery; The Director of the Aqua Park; Cinema City Poland; Hybrydy; The Director of the Jazz in the Old Town Market Square Festival; Lokomotywa; The Mokotów Gallery; The National Philharmonic; The promotions department of the Modern Art Centre at Ujazdowski Palace; The Guliwer Puppet Theatre; The Museum of Warsaw Uprising; The Museum of Asia and Pacific; Tygmont; The Warsaw Marathon Foundation.

For CAMBRIDGE PUBLISHING MANAGEMENT LTD:
Project editor: Frances Darby
Typesetter: Trevor Double
Proofreaders: Kelly Walker & Caroline Hunt
Indexer: Karolin Thomas

SEND YOUR THOUGHTS TO
BOOKS@THOMASCOOK.COM

We're committed to providing the very best up-to-date information in our travel guides and constantly strive to make them as useful as they can be. You can help us to improve future editions by letting us have your feedback. If you've made a wonderful discovery on your travels that we don't already feature, if you'd like to inform us about recent changes to anything that we do include, or if you simply want to let us know your thoughts about this guidebook and how we can make it even better – we'd love to hear from you.

Send us ideas, discoveries and recommendations today and then look out for your valuable input in the next edition of this title.

Emails to the above address, or letters to the traveller guides Series Editor, Thomas Cook Publishing, PO Box 227, Coningsby Road, Peterborough PE3 8SB, UK.

Please don't forget to let us know which title your feedback refers to!